Decode
the Deck

Decode the Deck

Find Your Path to Clarity and Purposeful Living

Daphne Wells, Karen Small,
Jessica Cerato, Beth Turner

Copyright © 2024 by Daphne Wells, Karen Small, Jessica Cerato, Beth Turner

All rights reserved.

No part of this book may be reproduced, or stored in a retrieval system, or transmitted in any form or by any means, electronic, mechanical, photocopying, recording, or otherwise, without express written permission of the publisher.

Some names and identifying details have been changed to protect the privacy of individuals.

Published by 8 of Diamonds Collective, Vancouver, British Columbia
8ofdiamondscollective.com

Edited and designed by Girl Friday Productions
www.girlfridayproductions.com

Design: Rachel Marek
Project management: Sara Spees Addicott
Editorial production: Abi Pollokoff
Image credits: Kolonko/Shutterstock (suit symbols), Francesco Abrignani/Shutterstock (all cards except Jokers), Uglegorets/Shutterstock (Jokers)

ISBN (paperback): 978-1-0688489-1-9
ISBN (ebook): 978-1-0688489-0-2

First edition

CONTENTS

Introduction: The Crossroads vii

Part One: You, the Cards, and Your Life Journey 1
   1. Why the Cards? 3
   2. Getting Started on Your Card Journey. 6
   3. Methods for Reading the Cards. 11

Part Two: Numerology and the Symbolism of the Cards . . . 23
   4. The Spot Value of the Cards 25

Part Three: Interpreting the Individual Cards 53
   5. Aces, Twos, and Threes: Self, Reflection, and Alignment 55
   6. Fours, Fives, and Sixes: Integrity, Evolution, and Realignment . . . 81
   7. Sevens, Eights, and Nines: Trust, Intention,
      and the Release of Expectations 107
   8. Tens, Jacks, Queens, and Kings: Opportunity,
      Responsibility, Compassion, and Dedication. 133
   9. Joker: Infinite Possibilities. 167

Glossary 171
Additional Information 175
Acknowledgments 177
About the Authors 179

INTRODUCTION

The Crossroads

Meet Robin. Her entire life, she has followed the rules. She went directly to university after high school, has a large social network, contributes faithfully to her retirement savings, and is climbing the corporate ladder at the company where she interned. She lives in a nice apartment in a trendy neighborhood and goes on yearly vacations. She is a dutiful daughter, calls her family every weekend, and flies home for the holidays. She has no problem getting dates, even though she hasn't found "the one" just yet; and that's OK—she's too busy for a relationship anyway. Sounds perfect, right? And yet . . .

Robin always feels this underlying discontent. She chases happiness and can never quite catch up with it. She is exhausted but will not stop. Because in her mind, she is always just one step away, one decision away, one promotion away from having it all.

She is very busy doing things in her comfort zone, keeping herself protected from failure and heartbreak. The ultimate multitasker, she creates duties to feel like she is moving somewhere, but she stays in the same place. She is too busy to tend to her real dreams. She fears they won't come true, so she self-sabotages and avoids.

Although from the outside, it looks like Robin is competent and put together, inside she is strategic and ultimately doesn't trust herself to live life without a rule book. She doesn't trust anyone else to do things because she can do them better herself.

The reality is, she is living by the world's rules, not her own rules.

She views success through external validation. She has done everything right, made a plan, and followed it—and yet here she is, imprisoned in the box she created. Robin blames the box, she blames the rules, while refusing to take responsibility herself.

She continually tells herself:

If only I made more money, then I would be happy.

When I move to another city, I will meet the partner of my dreams.

I've just got to keep following the plan, and the promise will be delivered.

But every time she achieves something she assumes will move her forward, the anticipated feeling doesn't follow. When will she learn that there is no prize for following the rules, that there are only more rules to follow? And that following the rules set by someone else will never fulfill her?

Here's the thing. Robin can wait until the Universe provides this lesson in a real-life experience, such as getting fired from her job, going through a devastating breakup, having a health issue that prevents her from working, or dealing with the traumatic loss of a loved one. Or she can take responsibility for her own happiness by finding out who she is and what she truly wants, understanding that this new approach will not shield her from life's challenges and will allow her to cocreate with the Universe.

This is the crossroads. It's not a point between decisions *out there*; it's a juncture where she's being asked to choose between herself and something outside of herself. The fact is, until Robin truly knows who she is and connects with her soul and intuition, she will never find the happiness she is seeking.

It's at this crossroads that Robin finds the system of the deck of cards that we describe in this book. She hesitates at first because she doesn't want to be categorized into a box, as she's found to be the case with other personality-type assessments. Drawn to the math and science underneath the system of cards, she reads more about herself, and instead of feeling constricted, she feels free. She is able to self-reflect and understand herself in a deeper way. Robin realizes that her main challenge is that she tends to seek external validation. Though it is hard to accept at first, once she does so, her path becomes clear.

You may be realizing by now, there is no Robin. We wrote this book for you because there is a little bit of Robin in all of us, and we all need to hear and understand the message that happiness is cultivated within. No one will deliver it to you on a silver platter. Nothing outside of you can fulfill you.

The deck of cards is actually a vast book of wisdom, a calendar, and a forecasting system that is a tool to understand and live your unique life. It was created for Robin and for us as a guide, and yet for so long it has been concealed. Upon the discovery of this system, it was realized that it held great power and therefore has been hidden in plain sight for centuries, under the guise of game playing. The knowledge was passed down only by word of mouth so that no written account could fall into the wrong hands and be used for nefarious purposes.

Numbers—the basis of the card deck—are not human inventions; they are human discoveries. We see them in nature, such as the seven colors of a rainbow or the eight legs of a spider, and they help us understand the patterns of life. Numerology is the study of the energy underlying these patterns, and the foundation of our book. Our book serves to demystify and clarify the deep wisdom within the deck of cards and empower you to follow your unique path.

Each of us found our way to numerology and the deck of cards on a different path. For Karen, it was an online workshop that unlocked a deep emotional response to seeing herself for the first time. Daphne received her first numerology reading and felt like she came home to who she really was—that all aspects of herself that had been squashed in childhood were in reality her strengths. It was a huge permission slip from the Universe to step into her power. Beth's curiosity was piqued after a casual conversation with a neighbor about numbers, patterns, and human behavior. Jessica was called to deepen her studies after a meditation into the Akashic records showed her a book she had written in a prior life as a man, and evoked the undeniable belief that she was meant to do the same in this life, as a woman.

The four of us connected at the start of our numerological studies, and as they progressed, we realized that there was so much more than what we were learning, and we wanted to dive deeper. As we did, we felt a calling to share what we learned with the world.

The truth is all humans share an innate desire for meaning, direction, and purpose—this desire is integral to our growth and fulfillment. Even before the four of us realized we had a specific path as shown in the cards, we were receiving messages through dreams, repeating numbers, signs, and synchronicities. All pieces to life's puzzle. This book will put them all together, giving you specific action items and a map with the most direct route to your life path. Studying the deck of cards can also expand your awareness and create empathy for the paths of others around you.

When we first embarked on this project, our intention was to bring a more modern, intuitive approach to this ancient wisdom. The only textbooks we were introduced to in our studies were written by two other numerologists, Grand Master Olney Richmond in 1893 and Robert Lee Camp in 2004. Both were written from a male perspective. For too long, women have been kept out of the equation. Our passion for this book brings forward this wisdom into the present-day Age of Aquarius and highlights a more intuitive approach, which is the way of the future.

And yet surprisingly, through the writing process, we made other profound discoveries. We honed our skills as numerologists and deepened our understanding of our own charts and paths, as well as those of our loved ones. We found ourselves supporting our clients in more meaningful ways. When we were able to fully resonate with the energetics behind each word, we unearthed the importance of intentional, precise language. Fun fact: Did you know that there is a unique underlying numerological energy within every word? Not surprisingly, this journey has led us to accept, trust, and connect more deeply with our intuition.

Since we started, much has transpired. We've transitioned from corporate jobs, embarked on health journeys alongside our loved ones, redefined relationships, and physically relocated to new environments. Throughout these changes, we've made conscious choices and served as mirrors to each other, fostering deeper self-awareness and acceptance.

Despite the shifts in our lives and our paths diverging in various directions, we've consistently prioritized this collaboration. Our commitment stemmed from a clear vision of what was missing: recognizing the power of understanding the cards for personal growth and our strong intention to share this wisdom from an intuitive, feminine perspective, making it accessible to everyone, not just a select few privy to its secrets.

Our commitment to this project is a mirror to our commitment to our lives, where collaboration and connection are cornerstones to making this world a more loving, respectful place.

This isn't a book about knowledge. It's about intuitive wisdom that's already inside you; this book will simply unlock it. We know this to be true because writing this book has unlocked it more deeply for us.

Although we are so vastly different outside of coming together for the writing of the book, this container created an opportunity for a collective of four women authors to cultivate a more intuitive approach to numerology and the deck of cards.

In writing this book, we at times hesitated to prescribe hard-and-fast rules for how you should work with the system. It is, after all, a highly personal and intuitive art. And yet, as with most disciplines, we must begin with some basic rules, which we do in Part One. After you learn to color inside the lines, you can decide to purposefully ignore them and go abstract. You are always completely free to ignore or change up the instructions; we simply aim to provide a place for all readers to start on level ground, no matter your previous experience. And so, with that, let's begin.

It's time to find yourself in the deck of cards and start living your life purposefully. This is not a book to be kept on the shelf. Soak it all up. Dog-ear it. Stain it with coffee because you're so excited to flip the page. Put it in your pocket and keep it with you on your adventures. Use the journal prompts and affirmations to spark mind-bending verbal-processing conversations and aha moments. We'd love to hear from you about your experiences and discoveries, so please get in touch with us at 8ofdiamondscollective.com.

It's time to create your own rule book. Let's get started!

PART ONE

You, the Cards, and Your Life Journey

CHAPTER 1

Why the Cards?

The knowledge shared in this book is inspired by ancient wisdom tracing back as far as Atlantis. Early mathematicians and philosophers hid an amazingly accurate system of wisdom in a form that could be passed down through generations, transcending the boundaries of languages and cultural landscapes. It is a fractal-based ancient calendar for Earth, written in colors, numbers, and symbols, that combines astrological and numerological concepts. The early adopters called it the Book of Life, and numbers being the universal language, the "book" became a deck of cards. Its purpose is to help decode your underlying characteristics based on your date of birth, and also to provide timely and practical understanding of events and experiences in your life.

Its potent nature encouraged the discoverers to keep the knowledge from those who would manipulate and misuse it. The Order of the Magi, a secret order and mystic brotherhood, was created and entrusted with the responsibility of protecting the information. Rather than writing it in words, they hid this wisdom in a deck of cards and vowed that it would be transmitted only through word of mouth. It is said that the original cards were carved on ivory tablets and used exclusively in the temples of Atlantis and that these tablets were later moved to Egypt. Years later, the knowledge was translated and printed onto what we now know as a deck of playing cards. Games were created so that if ever it was discovered being used, people could lie and say they were just playing a game. The evolution of the deck of cards has been documented in many different cultures.

At this point, you might be asking, *All that is really packed into a deck of playing cards? A simple, everyday item that can be found in homes all over the world?* If you aren't yet convinced about the potential power in the cards, let's break it down. The basic deck of playing cards echoes our modern-day calendar:

A Deck of Cards	Modern-Day Calendar Year
52 cards	52 weeks
5 + 2	7 days in a week
4 suits	4 seasons
13 cards in each suit	13 moon cycles
12 court cards (Jacks, Queens, Kings)	12 months
Face (spot) value of cards added together	364 days
The Joker*	1.25 days, accounting for the leap year

*The original decks (and old card playing decks) just have one Joker. It is just in modern times that manufacturers started adding two.

Although many different cultures and civilizations have claimed to be the inventors of the deck of cards, the Test Book, as it was originally called, was birthed by the Atlanteans. It was created over time, through observation of the patterns in the stars, the planets, and the actions of people in connection with these. If you are interested in learning more, Olney Richmond dives deeper into the historical significance of the system in *The Mystic Test Book*. In our book, we intentionally chose to focus on how you can use these cards as a tool to live a more purposeful life.

Each day of the year is associated with a specific playing card, called the Birth Card. Some cards govern only one day, while others are associated with as many as twelve. This is due to the underlying math of the system. Each card has a specific meaning, determined by its numeric value (bringing in concepts of numerology) and its associated planetary influences (bringing in concepts of astrology). While astrology is the study of the movement and positions of celestial objects and their effects on our lives, numerology reveals the significance and vibration of numbers. This book incorporates both.

From your Birth Card starts a path of cards that speaks to behaviors, challenges, communication styles, lessons, relationships, patterns, blessings, and so much more. The mathematical symbology of the system has the exact correspondence with the mathematical laws on which the Universe was founded. The original path, or plan, for growth was sequential—meaning we were meant to experience the system from start to finish, starting with the Ace of Hearts and ending with the King of Spades. And yet, life isn't like this! We must find our place in the sequence as it is now. It is the specific placement of the cards, like a finely tuned clock or precise calendar, along with their meanings, that provides us valuable information and insight into our life and unique path.

This is the start of your path.

CHAPTER 2

Getting Started on Your Card Journey

Remember: this isn't a book about gaining knowledge. It's about tapping into your intuitive wisdom that's already inside you; this book will simply help you unlock it—and, more importantly, apply it so you can begin living the life you were born to live.

A deck of cards offers a road map through your lived experiences. There are endless possibilities for which direction to go, which choice to make. Importantly, there are no "right" or "wrong" choices in your life journey. The cards won't tell you what to do. Instead, they are invitations for you to choose your own adventure. Finding yourself in a deck of cards comes with complete acceptance of who you are, and the experiences you have had are part of a bigger picture. One guiding you back to yourself.

You can use the deck to answer philosophical questions like *Who am I? How am I connected? What motivates me?* or *Why am I here?* or day-to-day queries such as *Is this the right relationship for me? Why are others so different from me? What do I want to be when I "grow up"?* or *Is there more to life than this?* The deck can guide you in all aspects of life so you can maximize what's possible for you.

YOU, THE CARDS, AND YOUR LIFE JOURNEY 7

In coming together to write this book, our goal was to decode the concepts of a deck of cards into daily practical use. We want to support you in a journey of self-discovery and self-awareness in a way that feels empowering. To awaken an inner wisdom that has been coded into your being since your birth. We encourage you to be in the driver's seat on your adventure of self-discovery.

HOW TO USE THIS BOOK

Take a deep breath: you are in the right place! Part One of this book is where we offer background on the deck and break down how you can use the cards to start knowing yourself better. After you read through Part One, this book is mostly meant as a reference guide. Keep it beside you so you can look up each card as it comes up in your readings. Before long, you'll start to get a feel for the energies of the cards and how they interact to tell a story.

To get the most out of this journey, we recommend that you use a dedicated card journal. This can be any kind of journal you want, from a fancy leather-bound one to a simple, spiral-bound school notebook. All that matters is that you use it! This will be the place where you can record your journey with the cards, creating a log of all your stops along the way. Throughout the book, we offer questions that you can journal about as you consider the energy of each card, how it affects you, and how you can work with it. Your card journal is a private place for you to explore, make mistakes, grow, and record your progress. It is a place where you will begin to make the practice of card reading your own and to intuit your own connections with the cards. Flipping back through your journal is also an amazing way to see how far you've come.

There may be terms you encounter while reading this book that are new or perhaps require clarification. We've added a glossary to explain what we mean by these terms and why we chose our interpretations.

In Part Two, we describe the numerical frequency underneath each of the thirteen numbered cards. Part Three offers a detailed exploration of each card in order. We've grouped sets of numbers together based on the themes that those numbers represent and their underlying energetic flow.

Each entry offers a foundational understanding of the energy of that card. There is no "bad" or "good" inherent in any card; you can accept the energy of that card however you like. Our intention is to instill potential and possibilities in how you choose to activate your energy—whether it is your Birth Card, the card of the day, or part of your life's path (see Chapter 3 for more on each of these). If everything is energy, the wisdom of each card invites you to interpret its message like a language, allowing you to turn feelings into words, words into behaviors, and the unseen into the seen.

For each card, we've included three curiosities—questions for you and your intuition to ponder. Start by finding your Birth Card and exploring the related questions. Answer them through journaling, conversations, or personal reflection. Or you could integrate this exploration into a daily practice: visit the energy of the day's card and let the questions inspire your journey.

Each card also includes three statements—affirmations for you and your intuition to reflect upon. Start by finding your Birth Card and exploring the affirmations. Write them down, say them aloud, and post them where you'll see them as regular reminders. You can also adapt the affirmations into a daily practice by visiting the card of the day and allowing the affirmations to inspire you.

BUILDING BLOCKS OF THE DECK

The first step to reading the cards is understanding the foundation of the system.

Let's begin with the suits.

First, there are two dominant colors used in the deck:

- **Red**, representing day, denotes an outward, *doing* energy.
- **Black**, representing night, denotes an inward, *being* energy.

Next, there are four symbols:

- **Heart** energy represents the season of spring, the first season of the year. It is an emotional energy focused on love,

emotional connection, and relationships. The symbol is that of feeling and reminds us love is the center of everything. The heart shape was chosen because of its unique combination of soft, rounded lines and a point; it is the widely recognized emblem of universal love.
- **Club** energy represents the season of summer. It is a mental energy focused on communication, knowledge, and ideas. The symbol is that of universal knowledge and can be viewed as a thought bubble or trumpet, depending on whether it is focused inward or outward. The clover shape was chosen because clover is the first to grow and the last to die, representing the lifelong learning energy of this suit.
- **Diamond** energy represents the season of fall. It is a physical energy focused on values, experiences, and worth. The symbol is that of reaping what you sow and can be viewed as the same from all angles, reminding us that there are many ways in which to measure wealth. The diamond shape was chosen for its symmetrical dimensions, representing a mirroring of your inner and outer worlds.
- **Spade** energy represents the season of winter. It is a spiritual energy focused on the unseen, intuition, and the higher self. The symbol is that of a shovel and can be viewed as a tool for transformation. The spade shape was chosen because of its ability to unearth the unseen, representing an invitation to self-reflect.

Finally, there are the numbers. The deck flows from Ace to King, with the spot values of these cards woven in numerological principles. Aces are 1, Jacks are 11, Queens 12, Kings 13, and the Joker 0. We delve into the specific numerology and symbolism used in the card deck in Parts Two and Three.

A QUICK GUIDE TO GETTING STARTED

The only thing you truly need to get started reading cards is a deck of cards. We suggest a traditional deck that is original and simple in design. There are a variety of brands, including yet not limited to Bicycle and Bee. We also suggest choosing a card deck that you will use only for this purpose, keeping other decks in your home for playing games.

No, seriously—that's all you need.

Our goal is to help make card reading a practice—a fun, contemplative ritual—that you will come back to every day. To help you develop this practice, the next chapter offers some of our tried-and-true tips. Of course, these are just suggestions. There is no right or wrong way to go about your practice. We encourage you to give these ideas a try, keeping what resonates and discarding the rest. You might weave in some of your own contemplative practices or personal rituals and experiment with how those might blend with and complement card reading.

CHAPTER 3

Methods for Reading the Cards

Now that you understand the makeup of the deck, it's time to begin exploring the deck for yourself.

There are multiple ways you can use a deck of cards to access how to simplify and maximize what's possible for you in this lifetime. One way is unearthing your place in the system through your Birth Card. You can also discover the place of others around you and how these places influence your relationships. Another way to use the deck of cards is to engage in a daily experimentation with universal energy and how that energy influences and relates to you. You can also use intuitive exploration through the use of card templates called spreads. Let's take a look at a few of our methods, which might inspire some of your own.

BIRTH CARDS

A great way to start out is to learn about your own Birth Card or that of another person. Your Birth Card, your personal compass, is here to guide you on your path to uncover the unique gifts, strengths, and challenges that shape your life's adventure. Much like the sun sign in astrology, your Birth Card is derived from your birth date. Although it is just one card of many you have in your birth chart, your Birth Card is your gateway into the system because it can answer important questions like: *What am I good at? What do I like to do? How do I communicate? In what ways am I being asked to learn and grow?*

Your Birth Card serves as a constant and reliable map because it doesn't change throughout your life. It goes beyond defining who you are; it delves into the deeper layers of your purpose, revealing why you entered this world and what you're here to accomplish. By tapping into the energy of your Birth Card, you gain a profound connection with others and a clearer understanding of your purpose. This knowledge empowers you to embrace every aspect of yourself, navigate challenges with resilience, and discern what truly matters to you and why. It points to the lessons on your path and encourages you to learn them.

Just like all energy, each Birth Card has a polarity—an empowered and disempowered side—and everything in between. As we explore both sides in the individual descriptions in Part Three, remember that embracing the entirety of yourself is the key to living authentically. When you choose to make changes in your life to honor your unique-to-you Birth Card energy, you will live a life of profound purpose, fulfillment, and connection. Let's discover yours!

Find your birthday in the Birth Card Chart, which is a visual representation of the underlying mathematical equation of the system that gives each card a unique solar value. You do not need to understand the intricacies of the system or the mathematical formula as you begin to access this information. (If you are curious about this mathematical equation, you can find it in the "Additional Information" section at the end of this book.)

For example, January 3 is the Jack of Spades.

When you flip through the following pages to read about your Birth Card, you'll see we've offered information on the empowered opportunities you have in front of you as well as potential challenges you may face. We encourage you to be curious and use the curiosities and statements to discover and embrace your place in the system.

The more you know yourself, the more you can love yourself. When you continue to get to know yourself on a more intimate level, you tap into who you are today and who you are becoming.

Once you increase trust and awareness in your own intuition, you

Birth Card Chart

	JAN	FEB	MAR	APR	MAY	JUN	JUL	AUG	SEP	OCT	NOV	DEC
1	K♠	J♠	9♠	7♠	5♠	3♠	A♠	Q♦	10♦	8♦	6♦	4♦
2	Q♠	10♠	8♠	6♠	4♠	2♠	K♦	J♦	9♦	7♦	5♦	3♦
3	J♠	9♠	7♠	5♠	3♠	A♠	Q♦	10♦	8♦	6♦	4♦	2♦
4	10♠	8♠	6♠	4♠	2♠	K♦	J♦	9♦	7♦	5♦	3♦	A♦
5	9♠	7♠	5♠	3♠	A♠	Q♦	10♦	8♦	6♦	4♦	2♦	K♣
6	8♠	6♠	4♠	2♠	K♦	J♦	9♦	7♦	5♦	3♦	A♦	Q♣
7	7♠	5♠	3♠	A♠	Q♦	10♦	8♦	6♦	4♦	2♦	K♣	J♣
8	6♠	4♠	2♠	K♦	J♦	9♦	7♦	5♦	3♦	A♦	Q♣	10♣
9	5♠	3♠	A♠	Q♦	10♦	8♦	6♦	4♦	2♦	K♣	J♣	9♣
10	4♠	2♠	K♦	J♦	9♦	7♦	5♦	3♦	A♦	Q♣	10♣	8♣
11	3♠	A♠	Q♦	10♦	8♦	6♦	4♦	2♦	K♣	J♣	9♣	7♣
12	2♠	K♦	J♦	9♦	7♦	5♦	3♦	A♦	Q♣	10♣	8♣	6♣
13	A♠	Q♦	10♦	8♦	6♦	4♦	2♦	K♣	J♣	9♣	7♣	5♣
14	K♦	J♦	9♦	7♦	5♦	3♦	A♦	Q♣	10♣	8♣	6♣	4♣
15	Q♦	10♦	8♦	6♦	4♦	2♦	K♣	J♣	9♣	7♣	5♣	3♣
16	J♦	9♦	7♦	5♦	3♦	A♦	Q♣	10♣	8♣	6♣	4♣	2♣
17	10♦	8♦	6♦	4♦	2♦	K♣	J♣	9♣	7♣	5♣	3♣	A♣
18	9♦	7♦	5♦	3♦	A♦	Q♣	10♣	8♣	6♣	4♣	2♣	K♥
19	8♦	6♦	4♦	2♦	K♣	J♣	9♣	7♣	5♣	3♣	A♣	Q♥
20	7♦	5♦	3♦	A♦	Q♣	10♣	8♣	6♣	4♣	2♣	K♥	J♥
21	6♦	4♦	2♦	K♣	J♣	9♣	7♣	5♣	3♣	A♣	Q♥	10♥
22	5♦	3♦	A♦	Q♣	10♣	8♣	6♣	4♣	2♣	K♥	J♥	9♥
23	4♦	2♦	K♣	J♣	9♣	7♣	5♣	3♣	A♣	Q♥	10♥	8♥
24	3♦	A♦	Q♣	10♣	8♣	6♣	4♣	2♣	K♥	J♥	9♥	7♥
25	2♦	K♣	J♣	9♣	7♣	5♣	3♣	A♣	Q♥	10♥	8♥	6♥
26	A♦	Q♣	10♣	8♣	6♣	4♣	2♣	K♥	J♥	9♥	7♥	5♥
27	K♣	J♣	9♣	7♣	5♣	3♣	A♣	Q♥	10♥	8♥	6♥	4♥
28	Q♣	10♣	8♣	6♣	4♣	2♣	K♥	J♥	9♥	7♥	5♥	3♥
29	J♣	9♣	7♣	5♣	3♣	A♣	Q♥	10♥	8♥	6♥	4♥	2♥
30	10♣		6♣	4♣	2♣	K♥	J♥	9♥	7♥	5♥	3♥	A♥
31	9♣		5♣		A♣		10♥	8♥		4♥		Joker

can begin to have a deeper connection with others. When looking at Birth Cards for other people, you may see yourself in their card as well. If you are finding yourself drawn to a message, it may be because it is in your life's path. Each individual card is connected and tells a story of your life, with many aspects that relate to your life's path.

It is important to note that there is no hierarchy in the system. There are no superior or inferior Birth Cards, only different strengths, challenges, and expressions. And in fact, if we live many lifetimes, we will eventually journey through all the paths of each card.

We want to be careful here not to limit ourselves by our Birth Card. Birth Cards are simply a part of who we are; they don't describe our totality. There is a whole system to understanding yourself and others through the full range of experience and potential. Your free will, the choices you make, and actions you take will always shape your life.

As you read through your Birth Card, we invite you to note which characteristics you are already embodying as well as any challenging patterns in your life, or anything that evokes an uncomfortable feeling. Awareness is key to your growth and expansion. Learning more about your Birth Card is the catalyst for this awareness.

ENERGY OF THE DAY

We've found that the true magick of the cards lies in their daily use. A great exercise to become more familiar with and unlock this magick is to explore the energy of each day. Since each card represents a specific day or days, we all experience the energy of every card throughout the year. This concept is called universal energy, and it's experienced very similarly to the weather. By reading the energy of the card of the day, you will get a sense of the opportunities available to you as well as the challenges that may pop up. Then, it is your choice how you will interact with that energy—and this will be different for everyone. It's just as if a meteorologist tells you it's going to rain: you may choose to bring an umbrella on a walk, while your friend may choose to stay indoors and your kids may choose to run around outside naked. And, depending on your birth chart, you will experience the energy differently because it is more like you or different than you.

Of course, there is more to your birth chart than just your Birth Card, and these additional influences also play a part in how you experience universal energy. If you are interested in learning more about your birth chart, we suggest you get in touch with a professional chart reader—any of us would be happy to read your chart for you!

Your birth chart is your map to the system. Similar to a walking route, you start with the You Are Here symbol and find your way through your life's path. Your specific birth chart points to the ways you inherently communicate, work, dream, think, receive blessings, face challenges, and navigate relationships. Each step and influence is unique and is based on the numbers, symbols, and energy present in your chart at any given time. The intention of this book is not to teach the entire system. It's simply to introduce you to the system and your energy, and to inspire further curiosity. If you are interested in learning the system and being able to do calculated readings for yourself and others, please visit 8ofdiamondscollective.com.

INTUITIVE EXPLORATION

When you know the inner workings of this deck, the possibilities of knowing more about yourself are endless. Keep this book beside you as you explore the cards to help guide your readings. The goal is for you to develop your own system for understanding the guidance of the cards, using traditional ideas about numerology and the visual themes as well as your own intuition.

Your intuition is a profound gift. The more you engage with it, the deeper your connection will become. One powerful method for strengthening this bond is through intuitive pulls. Rather than viewing this practice as seeking external answers or guidance, see each card as a messenger translating your inner wisdom.

Whether you are new to using cards or a seasoned card puller, we hope this section will inspire your exploration. Trust that you will automatically draw the cards that are a direct vibrational match to your current situation. Intuitive pulls are not designed to predict your future, but rather to guide you in creating the future you desire.

There are no set rules when it comes to using the cards, and you can never make a mistake. Your job is to get comfortable and trust that you'll be guided in a way that serves you. That said, we will share with you some best practices here. Build confidence in yourself. Every card you draw is significant, even if it appears to have no relevance to the question you've asked. Even though you may not understand the card's meaning at the time, pay attention to its message, write it down, and keep an open mind. Look for the bigger picture.

Before you begin, remove the Joker from the deck and set it aside; that said, we have included one intuitive template spread that does use it, so keep it handy.

Let's play!

Step One
Take a few moments to focus, clear your mind of distractions, and connect to the deck of cards.

Step Two
When you are ready, hold the cards in your hands, place them against your heart, and affirm your intention to connect.

Step Three
Your intention and the quality of your question are important. Take a few moments to clarify precisely what you seek to understand. Consider writing it down or vocalizing it three times to solidify your focus.

Step Four
Close your eyes and take three deep breaths. Shuffle the deck three times, then cut it once. Without reshuffling, draw cards from the top and place them face up in front of you according to the templates we suggest in the following pages.

Step Five
Once the template is filled, review each card's description

for its position and note what resonates with you. Then, contemplate the reading as a whole.

Things to consider:

- When you're shuffling or pulling your cards, if one or two happen to fall from the deck, be aware that this may not be an accident. These cards may require your contemplation and have an important message to share. Pay attention to their meaning.
- Notice the direction the cards face. For some, it will make no difference (e.g., Ten of Diamonds), while others will feel and look different depending on how you pull them (e.g., Ace of Spades), giving you clues as to whether the energy is more internal or external. For example, you can count how many of the symbols are pointing toward you or away from you. This will indicate clues as to whether a card is more internally focused (pointing toward you) or externally focused (pointing away from you). Most importantly, the question is *How does this energy feel to you?*
- You may find it helpful to keep the energy of the cards clear in between readings. We each have our own special way to do this. Beth stores her cards in a special canvas bag; Karen knocks on the cards with the intention to clear before using; Daphne has two separate decks, one just for her and another for clients; and Jessica places a large selenite crystal on the top of the deck in between uses.

Remember, intuition is akin to a muscle: the more you engage with it, the stronger it becomes. The more you play with the cards intuitively, the more likely you are to begin to see patterns unfold. It will be supportive to practice your intuition with the cards regularly, whether that is daily, weekly, monthly, or whenever a situation arises. Once you become more comfortable with the cards, allow your intuition to guide you. You may even come up with spread templates of your own and create your unique way of reading.

One-Card Spread

This is best for quick guidance, clarification, or confirmation, and is a great way to ground and focus. Some questions you can ask are: *What is my next best step? What is blocking my path? Where can I focus my energy right now? What am I not seeing in this situation?*

Two-Card Spread

This is best for connecting your action with the result of that action. Use this spread when you are curious about how to take action, the potential of that action, and what energy to bring to the action to get the result you desire. *What's my next step? What action can I take to support my next step? Where am I being guided?*

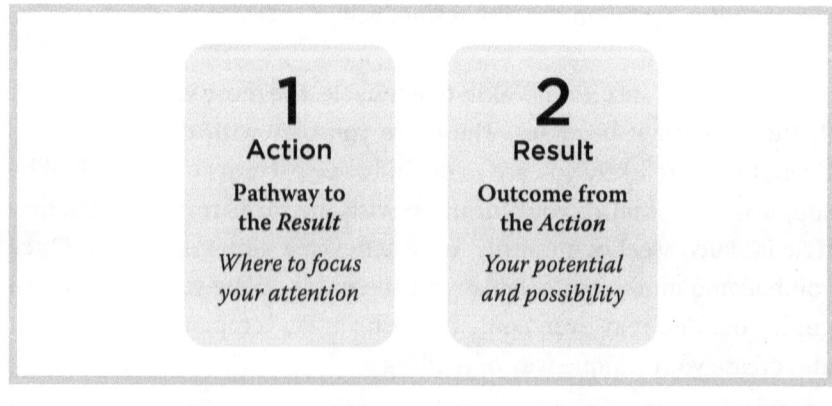

Five-Card Spread

This is best for when you want to create an action plan, yet you need more information or to see the bigger picture. *What do I need to know about this situation? What are opportunities I can lean into? What are challenges that I need to be aware of? Tell me a story about a current situation I am facing.*

4
Opportunity

An advantage
or strength to
help achieve
the *Result*

5
Challenge

An area that
will require
effort—yet
provide benefits

1
Big Picture

Overall theme
or context of
the message

2
Action

Pathway to
the *Result*

*Where to focus
your attention*

3
Result

Outcome from
the *Action*

*Your potential
and possibility*

Six-Card Spread

This adds depth to the five-card spread and is best for when you intuitively feel you're missing something. Some questions you can ask are: *What am I missing? What am I overlooking? What part of the story is not yet apparent?*

6 — Subtle Message
Adds depth and clarity to the message

Found at the bottom of the deck

4 — Opportunity
An advantage or strength to help achieve the *Result*

5 — Challenge
An area that will require effort—yet provide benefits

1 — Big Picture
Overall theme or context of the message

2 — Action
Pathway to the *Result*

Where to focus your attention

3 — Result
Outcome from the *Action*

Your potential and possibility

The Joker Spread

This is best for when you feel stuck. Place the Joker in your deck of cards with the intention that it will show you something. Shuffle the cards, and cut once. Find the Joker. The card before the Joker points to something you are meant to release in order to make room for infinite possibilities. The card after the Joker points to the infinite possibilities to explore.

Note: *The Mystic Test Book* points out that the Magi believed that including the Joker without intention would make "the readings null and void." And yet, why would the Joker be included if we weren't meant to use it? In our template, we use the Joker not in a position, but as an indicator of position.

1
Before the Joker
What are you meant to release in order to make room for infinite possibilities?

2
After the Joker
What are the infinite possibilities for you to explore?

PART TWO

Numerology and the Symbolism of the Cards

CHAPTER 4

The Spot Value of the Cards

Part Two will focus on the spot value of each of the cards—the numerological energy representing 1 through 13. Numerology is the study of the unique vibrational frequency of each number, as pioneered by the mathematician and philosopher Pythagoras. Although you may more commonly know numerology as using dates of birth as a powerful tool for self-discovery, personal growth, and decision-making, it is also used in everyday life wherever numbers are present.

As you read this section, we invite you to look at the cards. You will see that each card has been intentionally designed in a way to evoke the underlying vibration of the energy. By examining the underlying spot value—both energetically and in terms of how it is arranged on the card—you will begin to connect with the energy of the card more deeply.

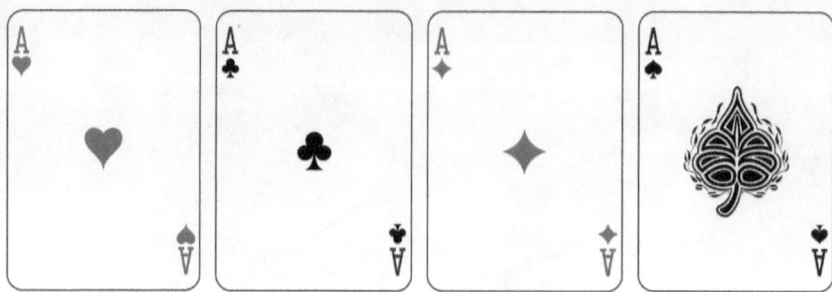

ACES (1)

The Self

Throughout history and widely recognized in card games, Aces have meant the number one, or in some cases, the highest rank above the King. The number one indicates beginnings, new thoughts, fresh ideas, and the foundation for how you interact with the world. Aces are the beginning *and* the end. Imagine a circle that represents a cycle. The starting point is also the ending point. Every new beginning is just some other beginning's end.

Ace is pure creative energy—innovation at its best. The Ace is powerful, driven to succeed, and proactive in creating its purest dreams and desires. Ace energy holds inspiration, is active, carries *doing* energy, and always strives to seek something new, a fresh start, or a new value system. Ace energy is a seed that has infinite potential when you are ready to work with it.

You crave a blank canvas, and yet after that initial excitement, you may get distracted by the next idea before completing the previous thought or project. You are independent and, when empowered, feel whole just as you are. Aces are the concept of self—your energetic being, yet more relatable; your true self and the self you express in relationship to yourself, others, and your experiences in the physical world.

How you feel about yourself and your concept of self plays a crucial role in how you learn your intended life lessons and evolve as a spiritual being in your human body, which you inhabit through your current lifetime. Your connection to self sets the foundation in all relationships you have: your relationship with yourself; with others; with past, present, and future experiences; and with your soul. Your communication, your ideas, how you learn and connect with all unseen energy, and your inner guidance system are known as your intuition. The more solid you are in yourself—the more solid your Aces—the easier it is to live in alignment with your soul agreements or life purpose.

When your mind and heart agree, you can live aligned in your body. You gain the stability to evolve and grow emotionally. This is only possible when you strengthen your self-love, self-concept, and self-worth and connect to the part of you that isn't ruled by the practicality of the physical world. Ace energy is the birthplace of purposeful living.

Although you can work with each part of self independently, it works best when you bring the four parts of self together: self-love, self-concept, self-worth, and self-transformation. You create more stability. This is to say that when all four Aces are solidified, they create a foundation for growth with a strong base. Only with that base can you develop and maintain meaningful connections with others and the world around you.

TWOS (2)

Reflection

Two energy is intuitive, empathetic, emotional, and soulful, representing connection and strength.

Unlike the independent *doing* energy of the Ace, Two energy is all about cooperation, reflection, and *being* energy. Two energy invites feeling and connection—to yourself and others. It brings together people, ideas, or physical objects, providing opportunities for us to respond or react. If Ace energy is self, Two is how we relate to ourselves in relationships, in our beliefs, in our values, and in our soul.

Mirroring is a key component in Two energy. The concept of mirroring signals that you are connected to a person somehow; body language, speech, or facial expressions are reflected to you. It's like when you enter a room and meet someone with crossed arms. You might assume they are closed off and don't like you, *not* knowing they just forgot their sweater. These reflections are nonverbal ways to show understanding, or misunderstanding, of one another. How can you get a clearer picture? You can ask how they are feeling or what they need to feel more comfortable. Asking for clarification can lead to deeper connections. Assumptions block them.

Another important concept of mirroring is the distance you are from the mirror. From afar, you may miss the detail or clarity of a situation; too close, and you don't see the whole picture. There is no right distance or perfect reflection; it's understanding that there are multiple vantage points and adjusting if you don't like what you are seeing.

Other times, it's the shape of the mirror that is flawed. Imagine a fun house mirror. Its purpose is to simulate the distortion of what you see reflected in it. If you are only looking at these types of reflections, you may even forget you're in the fun house and lose your true self.

Mirroring occurs in most of our social interactions and creates a perception for each individual in every scenario. No matter how hard you try to create one universal reality in every interaction, there will always be multiple variations of perceptions, and the truth usually lies somewhere in the middle.

Two energy can tip into fear and become indecisive, overly sensitive, and passive; overpowering, aggressive, and coercive; and everything in between. When you unify, make peace, and value cooperation, you become more compassionate, pick up on unseen energy, and create connection. You are in alignment, and can be influential without creating waves.

THREES (3)

Alignment

Three energy is the birthplace of alignment. It is where expression, creativity, and amplification come to play. In its purest form, it breeds confidence and expansion.

Intellectually, this energy embraces creative bursts and abstract, "outside-the-box" ways to problem solve. It is curious by nature. It is a wonderful world of imagination.

Three energy can be naive and lack focus. It can also be doubtful and unsure when the mind and heart are at odds with each other. When doubt creeps in, Three's creative energy tends to play it safe and steer away from more profound emotional energies. Why go through the pain of growth when you can just have fun?

When Three energy appears, it has the potential to mess with the reflection and connection of the Two because it wants to express and grow. Three energy wants more of everything and, more than anything, to share it all with the world.

Look at the cards. Threes are aligned down the center of the card in one single row, and yet the symbols are not all facing the same direction. Why? This brings in one of the challenges within the Three—indecision and doubting which direction to go or where to place your attention.

Where you focus your attention is where the amplification will occur. The Universe doesn't judge and will go where you choose to focus. When you compare yourself to others, doubt your ability, judge the speed at which you are moving, or lack focus on a task, doing becomes more difficult. Attachment occurs when you rely on any other external thing, person, or experience for validation or happiness.

Are you scrolling on social media and comparing what you are *doing* with others? Or are you focused on who it is you are *being*?

When you can confidently amplify and express your heart's desire for the physical world, that's when creative exploration and expression can have some fun. The Three energy represents mental and emotional alignment in the physical experience.

When you are out of alignment, Three energy can show up as doubt, indecision, and worry; it may seek external validation. Three energy needs exploration, inspiration, and experimentation to prepare for the stability of Four energy. You can do multiple things, just not all at once.

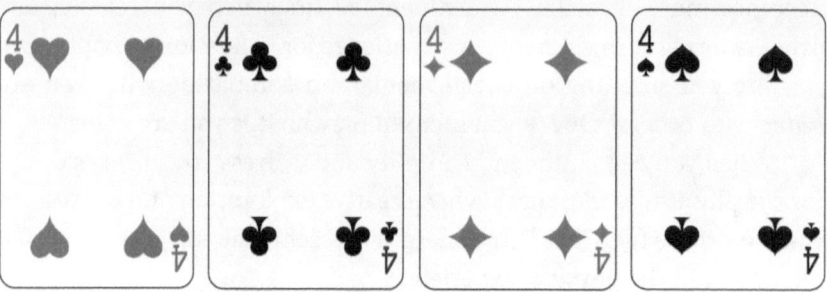

FOURS (4)

Integrity

The Fours are the combination of the four selves: self-love, self-concept, self-worth, and self-transformation. So everything that Four energy is, is created by you! Four energy serves as a foundation—integrity in relationships, beliefs, values, and expansion. And yet, one must not get too attached to the feeling of security that the Four brings.

Four energy sometimes feels like a comfort zone, filled with all the things, people, and experiences you are used to. Yet you must resist the urge to hoard or stay complacent in this energy. This is a table built to stand on, not sit under. And in fact, it's meant to dance on. And as you get closer to the freedom of the Five, perhaps the energy is more like a trampoline. It will support you in lifting off to higher places. You cannot have that freedom without discipline. Four energy is the discipline.

If you become complacent, this energy can be more like a constrictive box you are stuck in. It can feel as though the weight of the world is on your shoulders—and you may start to make decisions based on how others will react. When you understand that stability and structure come from within, you feel the ability to lead without the pressure of being a leader with a capital L. You do not need a formal title to embrace the "leader energy" within you. Without the pressure of a formal title, you are free to develop trust, confidence, and decisiveness—all things you will need when faced with the choices of the Fives.

However strong the table is, it cannot hold everything. It is easy to allow the table you build to become cluttered—so Four energy also reminds you to set boundaries, to keep the energy clear. You must create space to expand and make room for what really matters to you.

Sometimes we misunderstand integrity to be right or wrong or to be concerned with morals. This is false. Integrity is the state of being complete or undivided, an unimpaired condition. You get to create the rule book for your life and yours alone. The key to this book is to not focus on whether something is right or wrong; focus on what is right or wrong for you.

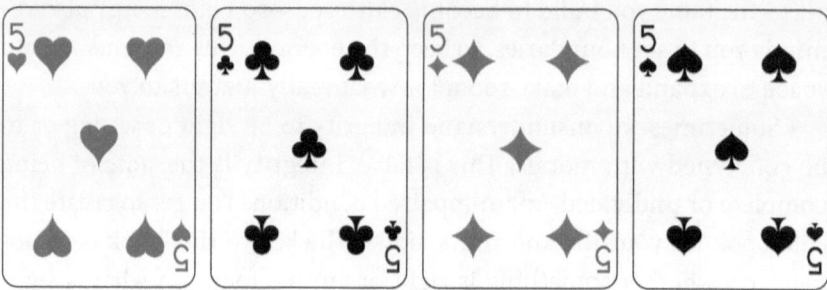

FIVES (5)

Evolution

Five energy serves as a catalyst for evolution, encouraging you to be curious about what it is you want. It is like an old-fashioned circular knob thermostat: you are turning it back and forth—fine-tuning—until you find the sweet spot. This exploration and constant movement may feel unsettling and tiring for some. *Can't I just sit still?* This restlessness can manifest in worry, indecision, fear, or lack of faith. But what if you could find peace in the exploration and trust the timing?

You like to do things your way—what you want, when you want, how you want. You are always searching to quench your thirst for curiosity, and you value being able to ask questions, learn, teach, and have the freedom to do whatever it is you choose. Sometimes you are so busy moving, on the quest for freedom, that you miss what is actually in front of you. You are so busy trying to bust out of the cage that you don't realize the door is already open.

Five energy is emotionally connected to all other numbers through the heart, which is why it feels so hard to change or evolve sometimes. Because you know that any adjustment you make on your end will also result in the potential change to others around you. Here's the thing: There is always the invitation to cocreate. If you change in a relationship, for example, it may invite the other person to change as well.

Five energy invites growth.

Traditionally, Five energy is associated more closely with change; change evokes a finite destination, moving from this to that. The true essence of the Five is ongoing, continual change; it is evolution. It's not about the destination; it is about the journey.

Five energy is unique because it is where the fifth dimension becomes apparent. It is multidimensional and multifaceted. Therefore, it is not the choice that is important; it's how you *feel* about that choice. It's not right or wrong, good or bad. It just is. Your evolution is dynamic. Because of this, we can't always be in perpetual change. It's like a growth spurt, you need time to adjust to your new body. Integration is just as essential as evolution.

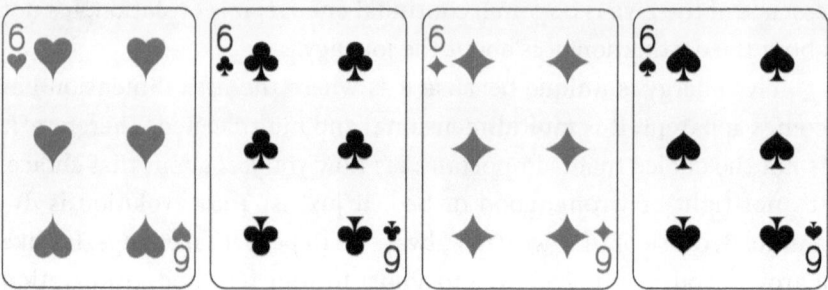

SIXES (6)

Realignment

Six energy serves as a reminder to steady the ship, to get back on your path. It is all about realignment; you need time to integrate. For this reason, Six energy can sometimes feel slow—like you're moving two steps forward and one step back. The less you are disappointed by this, the more you can embrace it as a dance and enjoy the rhythm of the cha-cha-cha.

There is duality in Six energy. Our mind finds it really hard to understand duality; it is hard to imagine that two things can exist at the same time—especially when they are polar opposites. What if instead of *either* or *but*, we use *and*? This is duality: the concept of two opposing forces or aspects that exist together, often seen as complementary, such as yin and yang. And yet, the most impactful energy of the Six is the duality within *you*. Yes, you have a strong mind, and your intuition is off the charts. Need proof? The term *sixth sense* refers to an intuitive ability or perception beyond the five primary senses. You innately hold this sixth sense; it's in your code.

Have you ever tried peanut butter and chocolate, cheese and honey, or watermelon and salt? These seem to be quite different, yet the sweet and savory complement each other. The thing is, you need to experience it to believe it. This translates to: You must allow people to experience you to get you. You must let them in at the risk of being misunderstood.

Six energy can sometimes seek perfectionism—after all, Six is the first perfect number, which is a number whose factors (excluding the number itself) add together to make the original number. (The factors of 6 are 1, 2, and 3, and 1 + 2 + 3 = 6.) And yet, this is also the perfect energy in which to make mistakes. As you step into realignment, instead of holding your mistakes with shame like large rocks, lay them down as stepping-stones to create your pathway to success. By definition of the word, in order to *re*align, you need to first become aware of and accept that you are out of alignment. Six requires responsibility; you don't have to carry that heavy load.

Sometimes, you try so hard to balance, harmonize, or equalize things that you forget about the flow. Instead of allowing your thinking to be so linear, you can benefit by learning the nuance of patience and allowing the integration to settle in you, at its own pace.

Six energy is a beautiful representation of karma. When viewed linearly, it can be seen as consequential or as a cause and effect. However, when you view it energetically, the Six serves as more of a guardrail. This means there is no such thing as good or bad karma; karma is simply the energetic boundaries that redirect you to get you back on track if you veer off. *It's not personal; it just is.* When on the receiving end of karma, you may fall into victimhood. Conversely, you may fall into being vengeful or judgmental—wanting to "teach others a lesson" or make them see that their perception is wrong.

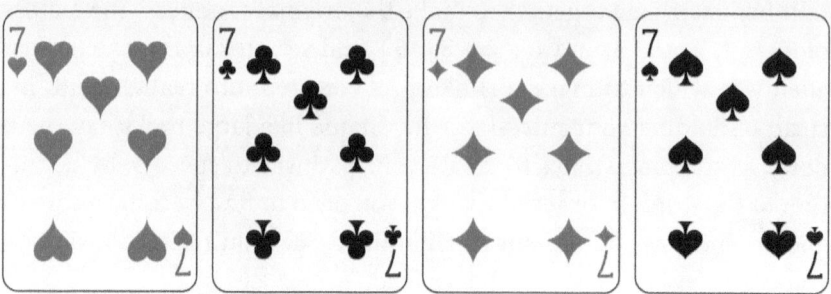

SEVENS (7)

Invitation to Trust

Seven energy can be like a smorgasbord of delights: What will you try or do? Seven energy is a choice point. It invites you to physically take the next step and trust while also detaching from the outcome. There are no wrong choices, there are only lessons. You learn, embody, and trust. The Seven asks you whether you are willing to take the leap and trust your inner guidance.

There is a spiritual aspect to this energy. A diving board is the perfect example of a choice point. You've climbed the steps. Are you going to commit to the physical action of jumping, or are you going to walk back down the ladder? This can feel unsettling because there are consequences either way. Are you willing to jump when you are unable to see what lies beneath the surface of the water? The choice is either to trust and jump off into a potential unknown or to crawl back to your comfort zone.

The longer you stay on top of the ladder, overthinking and circling through inaction, the harder it becomes to leap. It's not about knowing, it's about doing. Taking inspired action is the literal leap of faith. Sometimes you can't rely on logic. You have to choose based on what feels right instead of what you think is right. If you look around at others while you are on top of the diving board, judging their action or inaction, you will stagnate.

The invitation to trust involves owning your choices and their consequences. Seven energy invites you to understand and learn this through the four different suits: through your feelings, through your intuition and beliefs, through your value system, and through your own transformation.

In all aspects of the Seven energy, you will need to tune in, trust, and do. Reflect. Learn lessons. Then *do* again. Repeat as many times as needed to embody each lesson. Seven energy never stops.

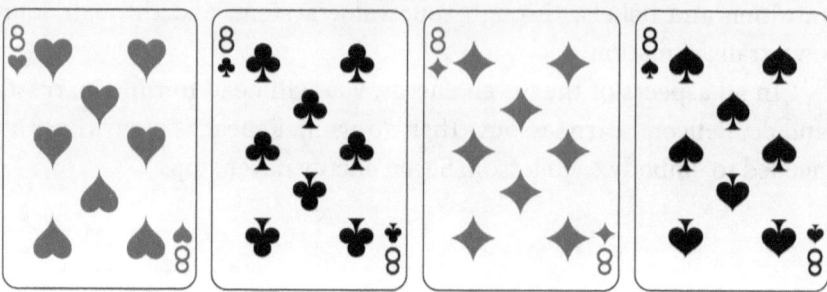

EIGHTS (8)

Intention

Eight energy invites you to flow with life and to become proficient in your focus and intention. You can choose to perceive life as chaotic or navigable; either way, there is no end to abundance. You can feel buried, isolated, and disconnected, or you can feel connected, engaged, and in the flow.

In this energy you have choices. None are good or bad. There are multiple lanes to experience. Just because there is a blockage in your path ahead doesn't mean you need to stop. You simply change lanes or adjust your speed.

The number eight resembles the shape of an hourglass, and yet inside, the sand is continuously flowing. When you feel stuck, turn the hourglass over again to redirect the flow. Your intention is more important than your effort to manipulate the direction and speed of the flow. That will only slow you down. It's like switching lines at the grocery store checkout, thinking you're going to get there faster, and you almost never do.

Whether your momentum feels too slow or too fast, it is not your business to try to control what the Universe is providing. Self-sabotage, procrastination, rejection, blaming, lack of self-responsibility: these are all ways that your need to control can show up. This is why it is difficult to recognize when it is happening.

If you tip the eight on its side, it resembles the infinity symbol, which represents flowing energy. Now imagine the current of a river: it is natural to want to go with the current and challenging to swim against it. Yet often, we make life more difficult than necessary by fighting against the situation we're in. Could it really be as easy as just going with the flow? The challenge becomes accepting the nuanced nudges of when to simply float and allow the river to help you. Trust it. The water knows when and where to flow. Your job is to focus on your intention, trust the journey of the river, and have more confidence in your ability to ride it.

Eight energy requires your presence and active participation. It is magnetic, and yet you have to prime your charge. When you hold too tightly or try to control the experience, you stifle your expansiveness. The more you relax into the awareness of your intention, the more infinitely expansive your life becomes.

NINES (9)

Releasing Expectations

Nine energy is releasing all external influences to connect into your deepest sense of self. When you accept yourself unconditionally, you embody this energy. When you let go of the burdens of "should" and "supposed to," you create space for new things. It's an important lesson in nonattachment: allowing what is to be. When you "should," you shame.

The part of you that desires expansion loves the release of Nine energy, and yet the part of you that fears change panics at the thought of loss and the unknown. Letting go of expectations allows you to work within the contemplative energy of the Nine rather than resisting it. Trust your intuition, and even if you wander, ultimately, you will find your way back to your path. You then have the opportunity to view life from a higher perspective.

Nine energy is objective. Mathematically, if you add any number to 9, the digits of the resulting number add up to the original number (e.g., 7 + 9 = 16 and 1 + 6 = 7), and when you multiply any number by 9, the digits of the resulting number always add up to 9 (e.g., 9 × 7 = 63 and 6 + 3 = 9). There is no exception to these rules.

Nine energy is a disruptor, a mess maker, and a cleanse all wrapped up in a pretty bow! It can feel like drama, chaos, and a whole lot of discomfort. There is always hope in every situation. From the ashes, the phoenix rises, and you feel lighter and freer to fly.

The choice is yours. If you fight against Nine energy, you still have the same result. The key is how you perceive the release: Is it grief or is it relief? When you accept Nine energy, you can move on to new possibilities. Your willingness to transform is the key. Every ending allows space for a new beginning.

TENS (10)

Opportunity

Ten energy offers you opportunities to share. How you respond is entirely your choice. You may feel overwhelmed, burdened, and frozen by opportunities; you may take the leap and accept them as they come your way; or you may feel an obligation to say yes when you really want to say no.

Ten energy is transformational—it's the connector between all the numbered cards that come before it and the court cards. As the first double-digit energy, the Ten shows the impact of coming together. The one says to the zero, *You make me ten times stronger*, while the zero says to the one, *Without you I am nothing*. Do not discount the zero. It brings in a spiritual connection and invites blessings and opportunities, along with increased responsibilities.

When you look at the card, you'll notice two sets of five symbols on either side, each one a direct mirror image of the other. This resembles an open suitcase.

Now, imagine a suitcase that you're deciding whether to open or close. Perhaps you believe there's too much in it and you'll never be able to repack it, that it won't all fit in again. Maybe it feels heavy, burdensome, and overwhelming because it's so full. Or, when you look at the suitcase, perhaps it feels as if you have underpacked. Believing you do not have enough may make you feel like you are underequipped. You doubt your ability.

Are you going to try to get in one last item and break your suitcase in the process, or are you satisfied with what you already have, trusting in yourself to work with what you've packed?

Growth and evolution have to happen inside you first before you are equipped to share your expansion with the world. In Ten energy, the focus is on how you mirror your evolution to others. Remembering the internal evolution of self that occurs in Five energy, Ten energy takes that beyond you. It's not all about you; it's about your contribution to larger groups of people.

You already have what it takes to put the puzzle together. You do not need any more pieces. Stop looking for more and appreciate your blessings. This is your time to shine and seize the opportunities. And yet, there is no point in accumulating anything if you don't share it. Just like the example of the one and the zero, life is sweeter together.

JACKS (11)

Responsibility

Jack energy, as the entry point into the court cards, is relentless—think young puppy, and restless; think teenage naivete. The exuberance of this energy moves everything forward without fear of what could go wrong because you're so focused on what could go right.

The role of Jack is to experiment with and develop responsibility in all aspects of life. Jack energy is physical and supports you to take action.

While all the cards want you to lead more, Jack energy wants to show you it can be fun to take responsibility. You get to create your own way of leading yourself and others. This energy can be creative and charming, resourceful and ambitious, independent and transformative.

Yet this cheeky, playful energy can also be irresponsible with a sense of arrogance. You might feel you're too good to be the newbie on the block or that consequences don't apply to you. Jack energy can be dishonest and immature, overgiving and manipulative, controlling and seductive. And yet, there might not be someone to bail you out when you're backed into a corner. You're being initiated. The crown comes with responsibilities.

As each is represented by a human figure, the court cards offer more visuals to unpack. Although the Jacks are portrayed as men, the energy is a beautiful mix of both *being* and *doing* energy.

None of the Jacks look you straight in the eye. Are their eyes on the prize? What are they not revealing? They all hold different weapons.

What do their various weapons mean? Traditionally, two have mustaches while two don't. What might that suggest?

Jack energy has huge potential and is not to be underestimated; the curiosity is in the details.

QUEENS (12)

Compassion

Queen energy is all-seeing and all-knowing; in this energy you're able to read any room you enter. You are assured and confident, with compassion for all, especially those you have the privilege to serve and support. Yet sometimes, your comparison or self-judgment can shake this confidence.

This energy protects and nurtures, trusts and supports, always with kindness. Queen energy establishes and maintains boundaries. You can deliver tough love when necessary, and when you do, it's a gift. Your intentions are pure and without ego. You stand strong in your power and use it for good. Queen energy knows that with power comes personal responsibility. How do you choose to use your power?

The potential for overgiving and self-sacrifice is present. When you start to view your privilege as an obligation, you become resentful and your compassion diminishes. You may feel like a martyr and become demanding and quick to react. It's not enough to just do; you need to make sure that others know of your doing. You are proving your right to the status by a self-sacrificing sense of duty. Imagine a fairy tale with a wicked stepmother.

All four Queens carry flowers. Flowers suggest beauty, pleasure, fragility, and the impermanence of life. They also symbolize your journey through life from bud to bloom—indicating potential, possibility, and personal responsibility for your growth. Because the Queens all carry fully open flowers, they wholly embrace their *being* energy and nurture with compassion rather than ego.

Their crowns are more decorated than those of the Jacks, symbolizing their authority and beauty. Their headdresses are a statement that they get to choose who they reveal their whole selves to—they are neither grandiose nor conceited.

The Queens are all ornate in appearance, both in face and costume. Do Queens adorn themselves for personal pleasure or external validation? Or is it to reflect their inner beauty and the beauty they see in others?

KINGS (13)

Dedication

King energy empowers you; it's the mirror for you to see yourself. You protect and hold space for others, providing safety and enabling trust. You consider the impact your decisions and actions will have on others. Kings lead, guide, and teach through modeling.

This energy encourages you to step into your greatness and hold power so that you can be of service to others. Be mindful: this energy can come out as demanding, overly dominant, overpowering, and controlling when you feel insecure and unsure.

King energy views life from a big-picture perspective and helps you see the full breadth of your potential. You are an artisan of your craft; you know you are the only one who can unlock this energy. Don't let this go to your head.

This powerful energy can feel like a heavy load; Kings model being born into their leadership role. A king gives his queen her crown; through this he models wisdom in knowing when to ask for help. You share the responsibility by walking ahead without looking behind because you trust others will follow your example.

Kings carry weapons that can be a sign of aggression or a promise of protection. Kings have responsibility for everyone in their sphere and help people to see their potential. When they knight others, they pass on a message: *I encourage you to step into your greatness. I see this in you. Do you see this in you?*

As a King, you have earned your stripes, having steeped in your lessons. Awareness is required to move into prowess. You have seen the highs and lows in yourself, so you know how they feel. You humbly accept everything you are: the good, the bad, and the ugly. You understand you don't have to be perfect to be a leader; in fact, you lead in spite of imperfections, or perhaps even because of the lessons you've learned from them.

Owning where you are allows you to move through your fears with courage and dedication. Where are you in your Kingly awareness and development?

PART THREE

Interpreting the Individual Cards

CHAPTER 5

Aces, Twos, and Threes: Self, Reflection, and Alignment

ACE OF HEARTS

Self-Love

Ace of Hearts energy, being the first card in the deck, is the beginning of internal devotion. It *is* pure, creative, energetic love—whether it is a desire for affection or self-appreciation, a new relationship, or even the birth of a child. It characterizes a surfacing of love or affection in one's heart.

Unconditional self-love is the first of the four pillars of self that create the foundation for growth and soul alignment. When you start anything, self-love takes consistent practice. Allowing love to flow through you as often as possible will help in all relationships. When self-love is lacking, one can appear to be needy or to be trying too hard to seek love and approval.

Before you can love others purely, you need to start with yourself. Love begins and ends with you.

At times, you may feel lonely, even when you are not alone.

Disconnected from yourself and others, you may try to change everything outside of you; and yet, it is the change within you that will bring you back to connection. When you suppress who you are, your emotions become a volcano ready to erupt. Letting go can release the pressure.

When you are led by passion, it radiates and ignites passion in others. You're not meant to think; you're meant to feel. Heart-led action is the only action for you. Step into your power and feel supported to overcome indecision and overthinking.

You are love.

Curiosities

How am I offering compassion and acceptance toward myself?
How am I taking small, aligned steps to create the life I long for?
What actions am I taking today to show appreciation for myself?

Statements

I am kind to myself.
Love begins and ends with me.
Challenges support my growth.

ACE OF CLUBS

Self-Concept

Ace of Clubs energy is the seed of intuition. This is where ideas, the longing for knowledge, and ways of communicating are generated. It's also where planning, strategizing, and visualizing stem from.

Self-concept comprises how you view yourself, what you believe about yourself, and who you aspire to be.

How you perceive yourself, how knowledgeable you feel, how you communicate, how you think, how much value you place on your *knowing*, who you believe you are, and who you wish to be are all integral components of Ace of Clubs energy.

It's where a yearning for information starts and ends. When self-concept is lacking, one can appear to have self-doubt, indecisiveness, the inability to articulate thoughts, or a lack of confidence.

When you do not know who you are, you feel obligated to try to be who others want you to be. People pleasing, self-sacrificing, and overgiving, you defer to what will keep the peace. When you prioritize your mind over your heart, love becomes conditional.

When you learn to trust yourself and others, you create opportunities for self and gain confidence. When you learn to love yourself and see your self-love reflected in your outer world, you become courageous enough to believe in yourself. This is the birthplace of intuition, creativity, and expression—it's never too late to be reborn.

You are wise.

Curiosities

How familiar am I with my knowing and intuition?
When do I make decisions based on the opinions and judgments of other people?
How comfortable am I with being misunderstood?

Statements

My voice matters because I believe in myself.
I communicate my ideas and wishes with clarity.
I nourish and build my path and write my story without comparison, knowing it is unique.

ACE OF DIAMONDS

Self-Worth

Ace of Diamonds energy is the birthplace of self-worth, physical worth, and your core value system.

This energy can show up in the physical world as a new job or set of priorities. It can indicate a yearning for more money, a new path, or an invitation to a new physical experience.

Your thoughts, feelings, and how you behave with others are closely related to your self-worth and value in the physical world. Self-worth is behavioral—*how I act toward what I value*, including myself. Self-esteem is also behavioral; however, it is a perception—*what I think, feel, and believe* about myself. Anything behavioral is something you can choose to change.

Ace of Diamonds energy is also indicative of your value system, the core values you stand for and what you base your life on. When you build your worth on external factors, your foundation is shaky. Your self-worth stems from what you value most.

When you are unsure of what it is you value, you hoard everything. You are not willing to let go, at all levels, and this can create doubt about what it is you truly want or what you bring to the table. When you're unable to see your own value, you cannot see it reflected back to you. You look outside of yourself for internal value. And yet, no matter how many times another person tells you how great you are, you'll always doubt it. You need proof. Your biggest lesson is that the proof is in the pudding, and the pudding is you.

When you are able to trust something without proof, you allow yourself to explore the unknown. The result of this exploration is a more honest expression of what you believe without needing proof. Allow yourself to go deeper in the unseen; what you discover might not be as uncomfortable as you expect. You may even find some diamonds in the rough and be surprised by what truly matters to you. In the process, you love and value yourself more deeply.

You are enough.

Curiosities

When do I sabotage opportunities that come my way because I question whether I'm worthy of them?
What are my top-five core values, and how do they show up in my daily life?
If I knew how amazing I am, what would I do differently?

Statements

I am worthy.
I choose to live the life I value based on what I stand for.
I prioritize the activities in my life that matter to me.

ACE OF SPADES

Self-Transformation

Ace of Spades is the card of transformation into a new way of being. It is the spiritualization of self and indicates a time of a powerful metamorphosis in your being.

What is a spade used for in our physical world? It's a tool for gardening; its primary purpose is to dig things up that we cannot see on the surface, to disrupt, to take out weeds and dead plants, and to create space for the seed—a new beginning, a rebirth. Make no mistake, this can be an uncomfortable and exhausting energy. And yet, accepting this as an essential part of your spiritual growth can allow you to navigate it with more ease.

If you look at any deck of cards, you'll notice the Ace of Spades is different. The spade symbol is usually more prominent and more ornately decorated. This is no accident. The Ace of Spades is meant to stand out. Think of it as a unique key that unlocks the magick within you, releasing your true path. It brings an end to something and releases a beginning more aligned with your soul. It unlocks the potential of a new creation and plants something extraordinary.

Ace of Spades energy can represent a need for internal work. Opportunities will arise in your physical experience, inviting you to do this inner work. Examples of this can show up as new work or lifestyle experiences, or can indicate health and general well-being challenges. This energy is similar to the stage when the caterpillar becomes mush before emerging as the butterfly.

Your inner fire is ignited when your emotional maturity is strengthened through self-curiosity and childlike exploration. You are more than just a physical being! You are meant to connect with your unseen support and heal from past emotional disappointments so you can gain a higher, more spiritually connected perspective of life.

You are connected.

Curiosities

When do I judge or criticize my growth?
What is my relationship with my unseen self?
How willing am I to dig up the parts of my
life that are no longer thriving?

Statements

I nurture my connection with the unseen parts of me.
I embrace both my inner knowing and my practical reasoning.
I trust and follow my gut feelings when I make life decisions.

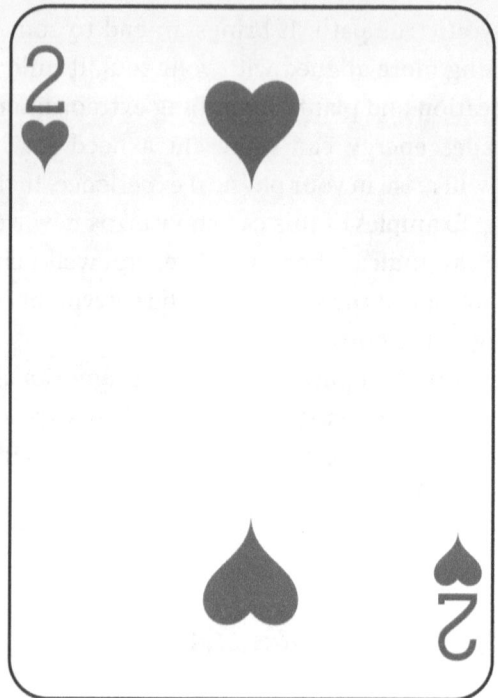

TWO OF HEARTS

Self-Reflection

Two of Hearts energy reflects your self-love through the concept of mirroring in relationships. The more you foster self-love, the more space you allow for your close relationships, and the easier it is to be aligned so that your mind and heart are in agreement. Healthy space or healthy attachment in relationships leads to clarity and emotional awareness of self and others.

When control is present, this energy can become coercive and overbearing. The need to control others stems from a fear of being alone. And yet, a healthy reflection of this energy brings in the possibility for new connections and relationships.

This energy is the origin of the connection; you get to choose how you show up. How you love yourself shows others how to love you; holding space for yourself in relationships is vital.

When you have mental clarity and fully embrace who you are, you welcome expansion, blessings, and opportunities. Don't let comparison steal your joy. Have confidence in yourself, your worth, and what you offer, and spread your love to others without conditions. Relationships based on mutual respect give you a high perspective, and maintaining emotional boundaries that feel right for you will allow you to shine.

Curiosities

Where do I allow appropriate space in relationships?
When is my happiness reliant on the condition of my relationships?
In what ways do I compromise myself to keep
the peace in my relationships?

Statements

I know that an investment in myself is also
an investment in my relationships.
I am solid on my own, and I choose loving connections.
The depth of love I have for myself is reflected in my relationships.

TWO OF CLUBS

Reflecting Beliefs

Two of Clubs energy reflects ideas and communication. How you express yourself reflects what you believe. On the flip side, how people respond and communicate with you is a reflection of the clarity of your message. Through increased self-awareness, you create more space for relationships that foster ideas, knowledge, and communication.

This energy allows people to feel seen, heard, and understood. The intriguing aspect of this mirror is that it goes both ways. Arguments and coercion can ensue when thoughts and ideas are too attached to outward opinions. The fear of being misunderstood can result in feeling the need to justify ideas and beliefs or shutting down completely.

Two of Clubs energy loves to process verbally with others. When this energy shows up, it may indicate a need for conversation that deepens understanding. This is the difference between listening to respond and listening to understand. A response merely serves to keep the game of verbal ping-pong going.

If you are basking in the ease of your comfort zone, you can fall into the trap of seeing things only your way. There is always more to learn. Be patient.

Standing tall and living a life built from a value system you are passionate about gives you the courage to ride the waves of change. Pivot with purpose, create inner balance, and confidently express your message; your voice matters. When you trust how things feel and learn to be comfortable with who you are, there will be no room for self-doubt. You already know who you are, so uncover your purest self and make friends with it. There is no need to prove what you bring to the table.

Curiosities

Where do I own my beliefs?
When does my want to be right get in the way of cooperating?
When I have a different belief, how can I communicate it respectfully?

Statements

I am willing to be misunderstood by others
as long as I understand myself.
I own and reflect my ideas confidently.
I verbally process respectfully.

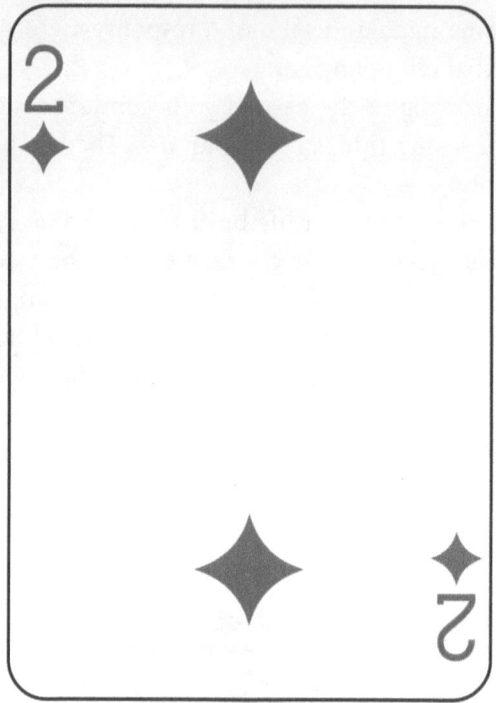

TWO OF DIAMONDS

Reflecting Values

Two of Diamonds energy is where the reflection of self-worth and values occurs in the physical experience. It's an exchange that has a material impact.

The more you value who you are, the more space you allow for experiences in your life. You see a reflection of your innate value as evidence in what you receive. This may feel like a harsh reality, and yet the mirror is here to help you grow. Like a mirror in a fairy tale, the reflection doesn't lie.

Two of Diamonds energy reflects experiences—whether that is another person, a job, money, a situation, or your values and what you stand for. If you're dissatisfied with what's showing up in your outer world, remember: it's a reflection of your inner world. The fear of not being valued leads you to *either* inflate what you bring to the table *or* give up your seat at the table because you feel you aren't worthy of taking up space.

When you are too attached to the external reflection, you may see a short-term gain through your actions yet miss out on the opportunity for longer-term impact. When you focus too much on the material transaction, it will leave you feeling unsatisfied or shortchanged. When you give your time and energy away for free, you devalue yourself, and others start to undercompensate to match your energy.

It's about being a good team player. Allow others to have their experiences while you have yours. Be honest with yourself: Are you hiding in your comfort zone? Or are you trying to control the narrative so others will see what you want them to see?

Passion and self-love are where the connection is for you! Honesty, transparency, and clear communication are essential. Take responsibility for your part in all relationships; this breeds compassion and allows it to flow with everyone in your life.

Realize your self-worth and the value of every situation.

Curiosities

In what situations does my self-worth require external validation?
Where am I able to see my value reflected in my physical experience?
When am I willing to recognize and appreciate the unique value that each person carries?

Statements

I witness my value reflected in my experiences.
I am open to receiving abundance.
The more I shine, the brighter the reflection.

2
✦

TWO OF SPADES

Reflecting Higher Self

Two of Spades energy is knowing that you are more than just your human self, increasing your awareness in consciousness. This energy is purpose-based partnerships and reflects your soul agreements.

Acknowledgment of your higher self allows you to make peace with your current state of being. In the duality, this energy can also feel busy yet unsatisfied; productive yet pointless.

When your relationship with your higher self deepens, your perception of your experiences can become naturally optimistic and full of gratitude. This new state then allows you to automatically look to find what is right or good in yourself and all current circumstances. You will find yourself asking, *What have I learned from this challenging experience, and how can it help me grow?* It's when the closing of one door opens another. Perhaps the job you didn't get makes space for another opportunity, the house deal that fell through makes space for you to bid on another, the relationship that always felt like a round peg in a square hole ends and makes space for a better fit. In these situations, you can't see what's possible in the unseen until you let go of the seen.

On the surface, this energy can also represent a work partnership or friendship that involves spending time doing things together. Two of Spades energy thrives with cooperation and joint effort. Strong self-awareness leads to strong connection. Attachment to who you think you are stops you from transforming into who you know you are meant to be.

Two of Spades energy invites a deeper look in the mirror because the reflection is of the unseen. You are invited to see your soul, to see the real you that's behind your physical face. This energy requires you to acknowledge what is uncomfortable. The fear of what you might see stops you from looking deeper than the superficial.

Lean into strengthening your communication with your unseen support. When you learn to let your heart lead the way, you can avoid the overwhelming noise of always having to make the logical choice. Making friends with your intuition paves the way to intentional living. You'll create enough internal space to see the big picture and will no longer be living in a state of victimhood.

Curiosities

Where do I connect with my higher self in my day-to-day life?
Where can I see challenges in my physical experience as teachable moments?
Where am I willing to accept that everything has a purpose for my internal growth?

Statements

I am more than just my physical self.
I have strong self-awareness.
I grow when I'm connected with my higher self.

THREE OF HEARTS

Alignment in Relationship

Three of Hearts energy is present when you *know* what your heart truly desires and can express your feelings to the world around you.

This energy offers the opportunity for you to amplify your emotional awareness. When you feel this in your body, you feel alignment and freedom from worry and doubt. It is emotional liberation!

Denying or suppressing your feelings indicates you are out of alignment. The only way to know what you desire is through experimenting in relationships. This takes time, effort, and courage.

Three of Hearts energy can indicate a time to get out of your head and into what feels right. If everyone were on the same page, no one would grow. The beauty of emotional growth lies in the complexity of emotional harmony with others; as with any musical piece, different sounds working together create a more intense and meaningful song.

Your greatest challenge is trusting yourself to learn as you go.

Where is your curiosity going to take you? Let go of "set-in-stone" plans; the fun lies in experimentation. Unexpected plot twists may test you, so try not to let life make you doubt yourself or what you value.

When what you do externally aligns with how you feel internally, your head can trust your heart because you know deeply what is important to you. You become more confident in your feelings and trust your discretion in expressing how you feel.

Curiosities

How can I explore and express my feelings?
When do I allow my mind to trust my heart?
How can I be aware when I am out of alignment in relationships?

Statements

I express love freely.
I release judgment and comparison.
I have compassion for myself and others.

THREE OF CLUBS

Alignment in Expression

Three of Clubs energy affirms that when your head and heart align, you can amplify your thoughts, ideas, and creativity to express your inner brilliance.

This energy indicates creativity and imagination, usually expressed through mental activities such as teaching, writing, or problem-solving.

When out of alignment, this energy can trigger mental anguish, such as worry, frustration, anxiety, and indecision, all of which can cloud your focus. This lack of focus is because your mind wants to explore and play, and when your overactive mind becomes overwhelmed, it creates uncertainty. When uncertain, you must drop into your body and let your heart decide.

When in alignment, this energy frees you from worry and doubt and strengthens your decision-making ability. These decisions create beautiful opportunities for self-expression and experimentation.

You are inquisitive. Asking questions does not create doubt, it creates clarity. Allow your curiosity to lead in conversations and discovery. You ask because you genuinely care and are curious, rather than just being nosy. That said, if you ever feel like others are getting annoyed with your questions, it may be because they are not willing to go as deep as your curiosity is taking them.

Lifelong knowledge gathering will feed your mental appetite if you can focus long enough. Knowing who you are and confidently seeking wisdom from within, trust that you know your stuff. Meeting new people and creating new experiences allows you to gain multiple perspectives. If you find you need proof of your wisdom, talk it out. You'll most likely surprise yourself with how much you already know.

Curiosities

Where am I decisive?
When do my thoughts and ideas truly match what my heart desires?
Where do I feel confident expressing my thoughts and ideas?

Statements

I quiet my mind so I can hear my heart.
I am decisive and take responsibility for my decisions.
I own my creativity, my thoughts, and my words.

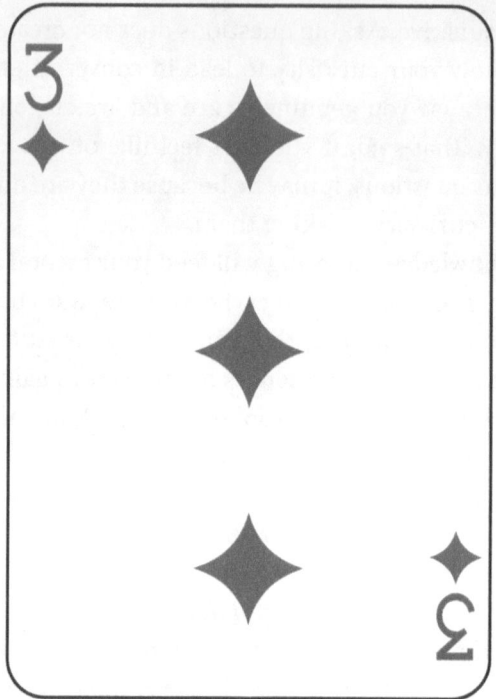

THREE OF DIAMONDS

Alignment in Values

Three of Diamonds energy is alignment and amplification in values. When you prioritize your self-worth and your values, you will create more of what you desire.

This energy wants to discover ways to playfully create something in your physical experience. Many times, it can be in multiple ways. When you liberate your mind from linear thinking, you allow your heart to connect with it to create and free yourself from limitation.

Yet, doing too many things at once can manifest as physical chaos, including hoarding, indecision, and financial anxiety. The key is to focus on your values so that the energy will be amplified.

The possibilities that can be generated when you allow yourself the creativity to play, to explore, and to think outside the box are endless. Your growth path isn't linear, so let yourself have fun with it. Give yourself permission to twirl, adjusting direction as the music changes.

Instead of trying to control the tempo, let go of control and surrender to the rhythm.

You may get caught up in imagining worst-case scenarios; a change in mindset will allow you to focus on new possibilities. Let loose; life doesn't need to be a grind. Unloading the mental burden of "shoulds" and making choices based on your values will prevent you from losing who you are to make others happy.

Your ability to roll with the punches is commendable, and the fact that you commit yourself to learning from all these experiences is unique. When you embrace and accept this unconventional path, it becomes your superpower. Transformation is a journey, not a destination. Your path of untraditional choices leads the way for others.

Curiosities

Am I motivated by money or by the joy of creating?
How is what I create aligned with my values?
Where do I need to get out of my own way?

Statements

What I create is impactful.
I am in alignment with my values.
I explore experiences because my life is in session.

THREE OF SPADES

Alignment with Higher Self

Three of Spades energy aligns with purpose, transformation, connection to your higher self, and unseen support. It is exceptionally creative energy, the gateway to empowerment, higher perspectives, channeled knowledge, and so much love.

This energy amplifies connection to the unseen realm and allows for the beginning of flow into a path of peace and ease. When you cultivate a relationship with Universal energy and unseen support, you will receive clear guidance to help stay in alignment.

As with all Threes—when the body, mind, and heart are not focused, mental chaos ensues, and the ability to make a decision can become difficult.

When this energy becomes too focused on the unseen, you may feel disconnected from the present, and chaos may ensue in your physical experience. This can show up as a lack of consideration for others because the responsibility you feel to grow and transform overrides everything else. Cooperation with others and learning how to resolve conflict through clear communication will increase confidence and keep you honest.

Even though you thirst to learn more, there is no need to justify or prove yourself. Your wisdom is conveyed through your actions. When you realize there is enough for everyone, you can release the idea that life is a competition. The more experiences you live through, the more you learn, so give up expecting a specific outcome, because that's not the point.

Three of Spades energy is similar to planting a seed and trusting the plant to blossom with fruit down the road. Release the anxiety about the lack of progress on top of the soil; a plant can only thrive with a strong root system, and that takes time to build. Having faith in the unseen will lead to fruitful creation. Your bounty will come with patience and time.

Curiosities

When am I connected to my inner guidance?
How do I connect with my higher self and tap into my creativity?
What tools do I have in my spiritual toolbox (e.g., meditation, journaling, rituals, movement, mindfulness)?

Statements

I am aligned and confident in the direction of my path.
I amplify the whispers of my heart.
I foster my spirituality while remaining tethered to the physical world.

CHAPTER 6

Fours, Fives, and Sixes: Integrity, Evolution, and Realignment

FOUR OF HEARTS

Integrity in Relationships

Four of Hearts energy represents relationship structures and their importance. You value family, connection, and friendships—and you like to cultivate a feeling of safety within these unions. This energy feels cozy, welcoming, and connected.

One of the most impactful lessons in this lifetime is the importance of boundaries. Setting boundaries, with love, will be integral to your happiness. When you set boundaries, you create space for your own sense of self to expand. You may sometimes hesitate to set boundaries because you feel you are keeping people out. Yet, you are merely showing them where the door is. Boundaries don't have to be brick walls; the Four is not a permanent energy.

You are loyal, sometimes to a fault. You crave peace in relationships and do everything to avoid conflict. And yet, conflict is how relationships deepen. There is discernment needed here: it's knowing when loyalty to others creates disloyalty to your integrity.

Although integrity means wholeness, you are not responsible for the wholeness of the relationship. Just because you invite someone to dinner doesn't mean you need to make the entire meal yourself. Share the load. Be courageous. Ask for support. Even though you could do it on your own, you don't have to.

When relationships feel shaky, do not look to the other person. The unease is within you; perhaps your integrity has been compromised. Or perhaps the relationship is evolving. Stability does not mean the relationship is meant to stay the same forever; it does mean the commitment and dedication remain constant as you both grow. And yet, commitment and dedication are decisions that you must make each day in order to cultivate safety and trust.

Curiosities

What part of myself am I shrinking to make room for others?
When do I seek stability outside of myself?
Where in my life am I feeling trapped in my relationships?

Statements

I am my own safety and security.
I bring my whole self into relationships.
I live a life of integrity built on a strong foundation of self.

FOUR OF CLUBS

Integrity in Belief

Four of Clubs energy brings integrity in thoughts and beliefs—you feel safe and secure when you have the knowledge you feel you need to make decisions. And yet, remember how you got here. You activated the Four of Clubs energy by overcoming worry or uncertainty about your ideas.

When you feel too attached to security and feeling safe, you may shy away from sharing your true beliefs because you fear they are different from others', and more than anything, you want to belong. It is important to own your beliefs and communicate them with clarity, without feeling obliged to justify them.

When Four of Clubs energy is flowing, it helps you to think clearly. Your thoughts are uncluttered and you feel satisfied. Yet sometimes, this satisfaction can morph into being so self-assured that you are not open to other ideas; your mindset is fixed. By staying in what you know, you stay comfortable in your box. From this vantage point, you are unable to see other perspectives. It is only when you stand up on the box that you get a fresh perspective of what is possible. The heightened insight invites new ideas and brings clarity and a feeling of fulfillment and satisfaction.

You like a plan, and you're an excellent planner. Yet, you sometimes allow the practicalities of life to override and control your emotions. Who has time to feel when you've got stuff to do?

There is a way to bring both structure and flow together, to bring the playfulness in with the preparedness. Trust that your emotions won't get in the way, that instead they are showing you the way. Life doesn't have to be all work and no play to be impactful. Giving yourself space to feel your emotions allows life to be more colorful and rewarding.

Curiosities

When am I feeling trapped by my own beliefs?
Where am I trading expansion for comfort?
Where am I willing to see fresh perspectives?

Statements

I create structure in order to create space.
I am willing to acknowledge other perspectives.
I ensure integrity by setting boundaries and
being clear in my communication.

4♣

FOUR OF DIAMONDS

Integrity in Values

Four of Diamonds energy brings a physical reminder of your values in action. You are aware of exactly what it is you value—and you hold a strict adherence to it. This can lead you to take risks in the physical world; it can also make you hold on to what you have for dear life. You may be afraid of losing what it is that makes you feel safe and secure, yet this is not possible because you can't lose something that's inside you.

Holding on to what you have only causes you to not expand into what is possible. Physical representation of value can show up in many different ways: money, possessions, position, or priorities.

It's one thing to have values, it's another to trust them. You value community and yet sometimes discount others because they don't fit the mold; you may write people off before you get to know them, and you may be afraid that others will do the same to you. The key is to trust what people do, not what they tell you. You must also allow your actions to speak louder than your words to be wholly you.

Four of Diamonds brings clarity of values. This clarity feels so good that you may want this for others in your life. Remember: Integrity is not right or wrong. It is wholeness. And so, each person must be in integrity with their own values, even if—or especially if—they are different from yours. Part of having integrity in values is accepting that your values are not everyone else's.

Your gift is in seeing what is possible before it comes to life; you must focus on the feeling of falling in love with your dreams, not get stuck in the details of the how. Trust your intuition and let your dreams in, without trying to control them. Allow your dreams to shine.

Curiosities

How are my values and priorities showing up in my daily life?
Where am I hoarding or holding on to things in my life out of fear?
Do I feel secure, regardless of my financial circumstances?

Statements

I value my integrity. I do ME. You do YOU.
I invest in what is important to me.
I am valuable because of who I am, rather than what I have.

4
♦

FOUR OF SPADES

Integrity in Purpose

Four of Spades energy is stability and instability rolled into one, because it is the combination of the seen and the unseen. Both have seats at the table, and both are integral to your foundation.

Sometimes you can find yourself swimming in complacency, like a big fish in a small pond. When you feel constricted in the space available, you will start to swim more slowly. It is at this point that you must decide to deepen and strengthen your foundation, because growth is inevitable. When you refuse to go deep, you restrict your possibilities. You stunt your own growth, along with that of others.

When you feel unsettled inside, it means you are settling for something outside. This energy can feel like a weather vane swinging wildly between all four directions, asking you to align your inner compass to your true north. You may feel satisfied in your work or fulfilled by what it is you are doing—and yet, you long for something more. You may start to crave change or feel restless; you have built the foundation and now it is time to explore and grow.

It is at this point that you know you are ready to evolve and change. Take a breath. This doesn't mean abandoning ship or starting over. It means using the structure you have built like a springboard. Get ready for the ride!

Although you may view creativity as a luxury, it is actually imperative to your growth and development. By expanding your definition of what creativity is, you will begin to see and appreciate its abundance in your life. Cooking, dressing for the day, styling your hair, planting your garden . . . creativity is everywhere.

You have the capacity to impact large groups of people when you value and love yourself deeply and commit to sharing all parts of you. If you allow yourself to follow your heart, you inspire others to do the same.

Curiosities

Where am I feeling fulfilled or boxed in by my lifestyle?
How can I be committed to integrating both being and doing energy?
How can I create a stronger foundation to support my growth?

Statements

It's OK to feel fulfilled and want more because
I live to thrive, not just to survive.
I live a life of integrity and am committed to my own transformation.
I give myself permission to not quantify my life's purpose.

4♠

FIVE OF HEARTS

Evolution in Relationships

Five of Hearts energy is about an evolution in your relationships and what it is that you love—including yourself. Do not allow fear or change or loss to stop you from moving forward. Just as you are evolving, others also have the same opportunity to do so.

Imagine an old-fashioned circular knob thermostat: you are turning it back and forth—fine-tuning—until you find the sweet spot. Release the need or want to control anyone else's temperature and focus on yours—even if adjusting the heat makes it uncomfortable for others. Remember: the other person always has a choice. If your temperature is too cold for them, they can put on a sweater.

You are an adventurer and enjoy connecting with many people. You are invited to break free from society's expectations and perhaps your own judgment of what defines a meaningful relationship. Do not let longevity define the success of these connections. Instead, embrace the moment, no matter how temporary, and dive right in.

Moving forward implies that you are leaving something behind—this may be true. Yet, you are forgetting that others also have the free will to evolve. Maybe your movement will be the catalyst for theirs. Or maybe not. That is not your business.

A new sense of self is emerging—and you must be open to changing your heart many times in your lifetime. This evolution sometimes evokes uncertainty. Through your uncertainty is where the possibilities are. The key here is to get your conscious mind to agree with this change of heart and, when you're ready, to implement that change with love.

Curiosities

How do I honor my need for freedom and connection?
Where do I allow my true sense of self to shine in relationships?
How can I honor my need for evolution, even when it could be viewed as shallow or irresponsible by others?

Statements

My relationships evolve as I do.
I encourage my own evolution and am gentle with my heart.
I allow myself to experiment in relationships.

FIVE OF CLUBS

Evolution of Beliefs

Five of Clubs energy is an evolution of your thoughts and beliefs. Sometimes, this motivation comes from a feeling of restlessness or anxiety. When you lean into this change, you will usher in a new way of thinking that is more in alignment with what you value.

You are continually searching and may change your mind often—which is why the lesson of humility is so important for you. When your beliefs evolve, it doesn't imply that what you believed before wasn't true. It simply means this evolution is bringing you more into the truest version of yourself.

Another important lesson is that it's not enough to change your mind—your actions need to follow. It really will be important for you to communicate with others through honest conversations, and to have your actions match your beliefs.

You get to fine-tune these beliefs through experimenting with what feels right for you. This allows for your truest expression because you simply won't accept anything less. Isn't that exciting?

Just as you grow and evolve and the seasons change, so does your temperature. The same goes for your beliefs. You must never "set it and forget it." Your beliefs are a constant dynamic that you must monitor—the only thing guaranteed is change. Allowing this shift and giving yourself permission to experiment is the difference between feeling unsettled and playing an active role in your evolution.

It is integral to have courageous conversations and share your thoughts, even as they shift and change. Even when—or especially when—you feel unsettled. It is through communicating that you become aware that you are settling for something; sharing allows you to feel more settled and prepares you for the external shifts you need to make.

Curiosities

Where am I avoiding talking about what is important to me?
How comfortable am I with uncertainty?
Where is what I've always believed holding me back?

Statements

It's OK to change my mind.
As my thoughts evolve, I am willing to adjust my beliefs.
I am open to being brave and engaging in courageous conversations.

5♣

FIVE OF DIAMONDS

Evolution of Values

Five of Diamonds energy is an evolution of values. You are a seeker of worth, in both the physical and spiritual worlds. The important thing here is to align them both. Do your inner values align with your actions and choices?

You move toward and away from things quickly in the physical world, embracing a hummingbird-like energy. You are invited to explore and experience multiple energies before you make a decision, like the hummingbird sampling little sips of nectar from many flowers. How interesting is it that when we see this in nature, we celebrate it? We grab our cameras and tell our friends. And yet, when we witness this in ourselves or other people, there is sometimes a label of "flightiness." What if we could view this experimental, beautiful, "I have to try everything to see what tastes the best" energy as a need, similar to the hummingbird's need? Reprioritizing your values *requires* you to experiment and explore. This is essential. Just because society wants you to stop moving doesn't mean you should.

When you evolve and move away from something, it does not mean it is no longer valuable. It simply means you value something else more at this time. And that's OK. Your trash can be another person's treasure. This creates a circulation and momentum of physical energy, the antithesis of stagnancy.

When you do make a choice and push forward, don't feel guilty for your past choices. This evolution doesn't change your value, it just changes the direction of your values.

What some might call flightiness is your superpower. Own your unique ability to trust yourself in the process, knowing this process is your life. Society is not your guide; your intuition is.

Curiosities

How did I feel the last time I tried something new?
Where am I uncomfortable with experimenting?
How can I reconcile my need to experience multiple things with the needs of others to keep me consistent?

Statements

I find value in every step on my path.
I give up good for the potential of great.
I prioritize growth and love to try new things.

FIVE OF SPADES

Evolution in Transformation

Five of Spades energy is an evolution in both the seen and unseen. You are the wanderer, reminding us that not all who wander are lost. Sometimes you teeter between three worlds—the physical, emotional, and mental. The key to this energy is to bring in the fourth aspect—the spiritual.

You prioritize freedom by continually evolving and changing. You value purpose, and when you decide to focus on it, you feel supported by the Universe to do so.

Trust and faith are important for you; without them, you waver. You may have worry, indecision, and fear about your purpose, and that may make it hard for you to move forward. This truly is the challenge of choice. Creating choices does not create indecision; it's just as difficult choosing between two options as it is between ten.

This energy helps to create new pathways—perhaps not seen on a map, yet known in your heart. For this evolution is not about only you, it is for the greater good of others.

In the middle of winter, it may seem like everything in the garden is dead. If you have faith in the unseen, you can rest assured that below the surface the root system is still strong. You resist the urge to dig it up to give yourself proof of that because you know it is still growing. So what can you do to foster the plant's evolution? It's experimentation. Does it need a bigger pot? A warmer environment? Pruning? Or simply patience? You'll only know when you know.

You may not understand why you need to transform or where you're going. There is no logic; your intuition is revving the engines. The water may be comfortable where you are, but its comfort is finite—if you stay too long, it becomes cold and stagnant. You don't know where you're going, you just know you can't stay still. You are the purposeful explorer, and the world needs you.

Curiosities

Am I willing to create more space to pursue my purpose?
Where can I give myself permission to explore more?
How willing am I to make decisions that others do not understand?

Statements

I need freedom to choose because choice is
integral to my transformation.
I pivot with purpose.
I trust that my inner knowing will guide me as I grow.

5♠

SIX OF HEARTS

Realignment in Relationships

Six of Hearts energy can feel like a warm hug or a choke hold, depending on how much control you try to exert in relationships.

Relationships call you higher—and yet, they also have the ability to bring you down. That is why it's integral for you to be aware of who you surround yourself with. Peace and ease in relationships are important to you, yet these qualities cannot be false or forced. Otherwise, this energy can create drama in an effort to break up stagnancy. You cannot hold on to someone who wants to veer off the path. It is important you remain autonomous; you can walk hand in hand with someone while still each maintaining your own version of self.

These relationships exist not only in the physical world; Six of Hearts energy is calling you to prioritize your relationship with your higher self. You are manifesting relationships not just with people; supportive energy is all around you, often felt yet unseen. Spirit guides, animals, feathers, songs, synchronicities like repeating numbers—these are all examples of guidance available to you. To fully embrace this energy, you must become aware of these forms of higher guidance and foster your relationship with them.

Because you feel so deeply, you may become overly concerned about the well-being of others, which can lead to neglecting your own needs. You feel supported when you can dedicate yourself to your values and focus on those. You may want to control through love if you have a linear mind. This feels like: *If I give this to someone, I will receive it back. If I love someone deeply, they must love me back just as deeply. If I don't allow myself to open up, I can never be hurt.*

You value love and time with the important people in your life. You find fulfillment in being able to harmonize seemingly opposing energies. You are caring, nurturing, and family-oriented. You are on a path of love and responsibility and are here to learn, and share, important lessons related to love, family, and emotional fulfillment. You have a strong desire for harmony, not wanting to rock the boat. And yet we all know that saying, "When this car is a-rockin', don't come a-knockin'." We all need a little knocking to go deeper and inspire passion in our relationships. So go ahead and rock the car, it may surprise you!

Curiosities

*Where can I realign and show up as more of
my true self in my relationships?
How can I be more open to receiving intuitive
messages from the unseen?
Where am I giving up something in exchange for peace and ease?*

Statements

*I move forward with acceptance because I feel at home in my heart.
I accept myself and therefore no longer need acceptance from others.
I acknowledge that we all dance to the rhythm of our own hearts.*

SIX OF CLUBS

Realignment of Intuition

Six of Clubs energy reminds you it is important to say what you mean and mean what you say. Because if you don't, this energy delivers consequences. These consequences are not meant to be punitive; they are meant to help you realign so you are ready for action.

Your mind is strong and so is your spirit. The constant back-and-forth can be exhausting, like a game of energetic tug-of-war that no one wins. This can be especially damaging when your mind takes over, because you begin to doubt your knowing. Your mind is gaslighting your intuition. You may feel like you don't want to say the wrong thing or upset anyone, so you temper your communication and then end up feeling resentful.

Words and communication are very important to the Six of Clubs energy. Are you allowing yourself to become a vessel for higher knowledge, or are you not listening to the messages your intuition is whispering? Your intuition whispers because it is not fearful or forceful. Your ego can be, and that is why it shouts. You are a seer/knower, often able to discern truths that others are not fully able to see. It may feel uncomfortable to speak this truth because it creates a sense of disharmony in others.

Sometimes when your creative energy hits, you start out with a burst of enthusiasm and effort, yet if what you are creating doesn't materialize quickly you may abandon that idea without really giving it a chance to develop. Your intuition is so strong and your creative ideas so progressive that sometimes they come before others are ready to receive them. Don't give up, don't stop—your intuition will know what path to take. Returns aren't linear; sometimes you will receive feedback from others or the Universe that what you did years ago made a difference. Like an imprint on the soul. You share your ideas because they will help the world, not just you.

The present moment, especially when it comes to your intuition, is important. Be in the now. Act on your intuition in the moment. This is the realignment. It is up to you to decide how you respond to it. Your return on realignment is an open channel, free-flowing intuitive wisdom at your fingertips. Once you accept this channel as truth, your spirit becomes stronger and your mind goes along for the ride.

Curiosities

Where am I allowing my intuition to guide me in the present moment?
When am I ignoring my intuition and why?
How can I create more quiet spaciousness
to hear and feel my intuition?

Statements

My thoughts, words, and intuition are all aligned.
I say what I mean, and I mean what I say.
Accepting the past allows me to write a new future.

6♣

SIX OF DIAMONDS

Realignment of Values

Six of Diamonds energy reminds you of the importance of taking things one step at a time. Although you may want to know what will happen ten steps ahead, by focusing on that you may miss out on the endless possibilities that are present now. Think of it like a partner dance: if you are focusing on your last step or your next move instead of the one your body is making now, some toes may get stepped on.

As your values become realigned, you realize that life is neither tit-for-tat nor linear. Can you simply allow yourself to receive without immediately trying to figure out how to pay it back? Conversely, can you "overpay" and not expect to be paid back?

The temptation to seek perfection may ask you to prove your value. Instead of proving your value, can you simply accept that you are valuable? You may tend to overgive of yourself to earn your keep. What if there were nothing to earn? This energy is a reminder to realign with your own innate value.

The end result is not always zero-sum. If you try to maintain that, you miss out on the possibilities and perhaps become engaged in a power struggle. Remember: the point of possibility is always in the present moment.

Your biggest lesson is about making decisions; you will continue to be confronted with difficult decisions to help you grow. Embrace the awareness that you can never choose incorrectly; you can only learn. You are here to work through issues of perfectionism, self-doubt, and a strong sense of idealism.

Passion is your life's blood, so when you feel a lack of purpose, you can become disheartened. It is hard for you to slow down and do anything *just because*. Expressing your emotions through physical activity or creative output is crucial to your well-being.

Spirituality is often the missing piece to your life puzzle. You can feel dependent on others and outside influences for your sense of stability, recognition, and love until you are aware and begin to partner with your higher self, your intuition. This connection will break you through to realizing your purpose in this lifetime. You will find that you are deeply connected, and this connection will influence your results almost immediately.

Curiosities

When do I see and accept my own value?
How can I remain optimistic, despite material circumstances?
Where am I unwilling to take responsibility for my choices?

Statements

I am content in the present moment.
I take responsibility for my physical experience by ensuring that my actions are in alignment with my values.
There are no mistakes, only opportunities to learn.

SIX OF SPADES

Realignment in Transformation

Six of Spades energy is a harmonizer, integrating the evolution that came as a result of your wandering. This is the realignment. Your growth must be in the direction of your spirituality and of your higher purpose. You are here to bring others to the light—this is why you get bored with topics that don't interest you.

The Universe is intent on making sure you are ready before you take the next step; if you step out of line, this energy, more than any others, will bring you back with natural consequences. Think of it like a course correction. It's not meant to be punitive, although sometimes it feels like the Universe is trying to teach you a lesson.

Six of Spades energy comes as flashes of knowing. Close your eyes and you might miss it! Every flash is an opportunity to fine-tune your awareness. Therefore, you must be ready to take the next step at any moment. Although you sometimes feel stuck in monotony, it's simply a delay. It will do you no good to rush or force. The pause is as necessary as the progression.

Timing is everything. Imagine yourself on a dance floor. One song has just ended, and you stand in silence waiting for the next tune to drop. In this moment, there is no guarantee of what is next. You may not know the song, you may not know the dance, yet if you are willing to stay on the dance floor, it will all work out. The pause in the music is not an indication to come off the dance floor; rather, it is a reminder to stay in the moment, however uncomfortable, and be ready to continue when the music picks up again.

This energy reminds you that growth is not linear, and transformation occurs at different rates. You can't rush the music, skip songs, or dance for someone else. Instead of spending the dance hoping for the next song, allow the music of the present moment to wash over you.

You go so deep that others may not understand you. Yet that doesn't make them shallow. Finding the language for your intuition is important so you can communicate what you know with others, ensuring nothing gets lost in translation.

Messages come to you in many different forms. Tastes, smells, visions, flashes of inspiration—so many pieces to the puzzle, it sometimes feels hard to fit them together. And yet, when you do, the result is miraculous, more intricate than anything you could have ever imagined. Trust that you have what it takes to figure it out.

Curiosities

When do I allow myself to get distracted
by things in the physical world?
When do I focus so much on harmony that I get complacent?
How do I feel about natural consequences?

Statements

In order to pursue my purpose, I first need to be aware of and accept it.
My actions, thoughts, emotions, and spiritual
connections are all aligned.
I am following my inner compass and transforming at my own pace.

CHAPTER 7

Sevens, Eights, and Nines: Trust, Intention, and the Release of Expectations

SEVEN OF HEARTS

Invitation to Trust in Relationships

Seven of Hearts energy is inviting you to trust yourself to show up as yourself in relationships, regardless of what happens. This trust in yourself can eventually allow you to trust in others, yet it is a step that cannot be skipped.

The more you learn to embrace your passions, your relationships, and all aspects of life that you love, the more you can detach from the outcome and potential judgment from others. This can seem impulsive from an outsider's perspective, yet letting go of this judgment is part of the emotional growth.

Seven of Hearts energy invites you to witness how you show up in relationships so you can learn that any feelings of failure, betrayal, loneliness, loss, or victimization are yours. The choice point of this energy is deciding what you are going to do with those feelings. If you can use these emotions as important teachers, you can learn the ultimate lesson of this energy, which is the importance of loving without conditions.

Just as with trust, unconditional love must first be of yourself. This trust cannot be outsourced. You cannot outrun the storm or rely on someone else's cautionary tale—you must experience your lesson firsthand, many times by walking directly through it.

This energy invites you to come into each relationship without attaching biases or expectations from past emotional experiences. In this way, you can experience true emotional liberation and the freedom to be fully seen and loved. When you're unconditionally all in and leave nothing aside, your potential to experience love transcends ego. Relationships are your ultimate playground.

Curiosities

How can I deepen trust in myself and in my relationships?
How do I show myself unconditional love,
even when I'm not feeling lovable?
How can I trust that others will still love me
if I show up as my whole self?

Statements

Trust and love begin within me.
I trust myself in relationships to love without conditions.
I am taking a leap of faith and trusting I can
navigate regardless of the outcome.

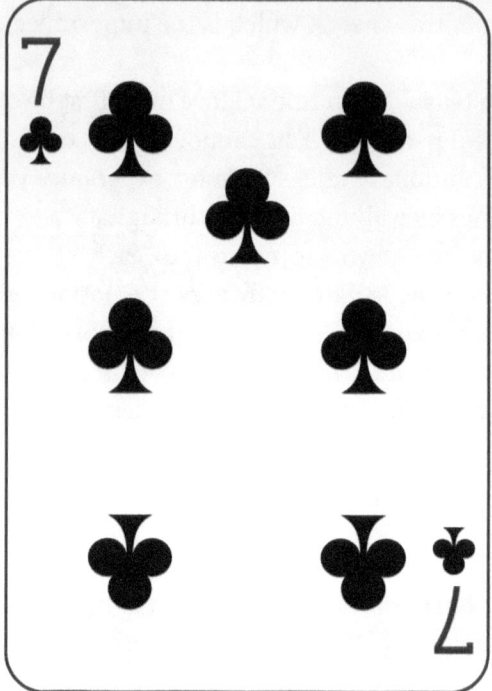

SEVEN OF CLUBS

Invitation to Trust Your Wisdom

Seven of Clubs energy invites you to trust your inner wisdom and to flow that wisdom into the world. Your inner wisdom is your most important teacher. You may be tested by others who require proof. They may not understand you or may wonder how and why you know. Resist the urge to provide proof. Instead, allow the wisdom to flow through you and trust in yourself as a teacher. Rest assured that for those who believe, no proof is necessary; for those who don't believe, no proof is possible. Save your breath.

You may feel the need to acquire knowledge so that you can teach others, yet you must first learn to trust yourself. The truth has been in you all along; the invitation is to trust your knowing, to trust your intuition, to take the time to lean into your inner wisdom. You are the wisdom you seek.

Sometimes you get so caught up in your thirst for knowledge that you ignore your own wisdom. When you doubt yourself, you may feel the urge to "answer shop"—to look for confirmation of what you already believe. You wait to do things until you know for sure or receive external validation, such as in the form of a certification or letters behind your name. While these types of recognition have their time and place, true learning is earned through doing, not consuming knowledge.

The kind of knowing of the Seven of Clubs is a feeling in the heart rather than intellectual knowledge. Rather than question your wisdom, trust it.

Curiosities

Where am I tempted to get stuck in a learning loop? How can I get out of this loop?
How am I allowing my wisdom to flow?
When am I trusting myself to learn as I go?

Statements

The wisdom I seek is within me.
Inspired action guides me.
I know my truth, and I do not need anyone else to confirm it.

SEVEN OF DIAMONDS

Invitation to Trust Your Values

Seven of Diamonds energy invites you to trust your value system, take action based on your values, and pause to reflect to gain clarity. Or is it the other way around? That is up to your individual circumstance. Remember: it is important to separate your inherent value from your value system. Your worth does not depend on the outcome of the actions you take.

    This energy can feel conditional or unconditional in situations where you are reluctant to act: *I am giving this to you because I want to* versus *I am giving this to you because I want something.* This dichotomy can show up in the physical results of your actions; however, you are not taking action to secure specific results. Give yourself permission to trust and step courageously in the direction of your dreams. Believe you can reach higher, do better, become more. Generosity must be shown without conditions, and it also must be shown without expectations.

If you're not taking action, it can feel as though you're living in lack. You might be pacifying this feeling through hoarding or overconsumption. Are you questioning or trusting your resourcefulness?

You go back and forth between wanting to exist and play in the physical world and wanting to retreat from it. You either want it all or you want nothing. The lesson here is to have the experience of wealth, not be obsessed with it. Wealth can be defined in many ways; everything has a price. It's not all about the money.

This is a highly resourceful, confident energy. There is physical feedback based on your action. You can use this as evidence to learn from and inform your next step. Even though you must not be attached to the outcome, there is a cause and effect in this energy. You get back what you put in.

Seven of Diamonds energy sometimes tricks you into needing to know the how, or have confirmation of results, before you take action. And yet, the lesson here is that when you know what you are capable of, you can trust yourself to navigate any physical experience without knowing how it will turn out.

Curiosities

When am I looking for validation in the outcome of my actions?
Where am I walking the line between reckless and risky?
How does my attachment to specific outcomes affect my actions?

Statements

I trust my resourcefulness.
I am embodying my value system.
I detach from the outcome so that I can focus on the action.

SEVEN OF SPADES

Invitation to Trust Your Transformation

Seven of Spades energy is an invitation to trust your growth and transformation. This can be in any aspect of your journey, including self-awareness, career, health, and relationships.

This energy invites you to trust your spiritual self with limitless opportunities to transform. When you trust the Universe to guide and provide, you expand your capacity to take inspired action.

This energy can feel abstract at times. You are thirsty for transformation. You can feel insecure and helpless, wondering whether down is up and up is down. It is an invitation to try new things and feel into what is right for you. Only experience can provide learning opportunities about the seen and the unseen.

Imagine yourself on a diving board that is not over the safe container of a pool; rather, it is above the dark, murky, and mysterious unknown of the ocean. This energy invites the action of leaping *and* navigating the uncharted waters once you dive in. It's being OK with the discomfort of not knowing what you can't see. Trust that you can swim.

This energy is a devotional practice of awareness, action, reflection, accountability, and growth. By being more of your true expression, you are teaching others they can do the same. These acts of bravery include peeling the layers of old patterning and society-imposed constructs. Being the first in your family to get divorced; quitting your corporate job to pursue your passion; choosing to have open relationships rather than being married; selling the family home in a thriving housing market to move to a more remote seaside property. These are all examples of how we, the authors, have embraced this energy. When you do this for yourself, you are extending the invitation for others to trust their own transformation.

Curiosities

What part of my life is inviting me to take a leap of faith?
Where am I hesitating to transform?
How can I be more aware of the hidden lessons
that my experience provides?

Statements

I am learning through doing.
I am trusting my transformation.
I trust that my capacity to transform is limitless.

7 ♠

EIGHT OF HEARTS

Intention in Relationships

Eight of Hearts energy is the intention that you bring to your relationships.

This energy brings an emotional maturity that originates through your connection to self. The more you understand yourself, the more you are able to understand and accept others. When you feel safe and secure in yourself, you feel safe and secure in the world. When you accept yourself, you accept others.

The next step to navigate is deciding where and when you will place your intention. Will you invest your energy into drama? Will you find peace within?

When you try to control, influence, or manipulate others, you are disconnecting from yourself. You are not trusting that every experience has value. When things don't go your way, you may perceive that as a setback. While challenging in the moment, these experiences provide you with new tools to navigate future emotional experiences.

The number eight is the only number that has no beginning and no end—it flows. When you disconnect from your authentic self, you break the flow of intention and you can feel lost. You search for validation outside of yourself and become emotionally reliant on others. The connected self feels full of life, charming, loving, and divinely guided. The disconnected self feels alone, like the black sheep of the flock, an outsider, out of place.

This is community energy that requires discernment between fitting in and belonging. Fitting in implies you are constricting yourself and controlling how you show up in order to be accepted. Belonging means there is a place for you exactly as you are. When you intentionally belong with yourself, you belong anywhere and everywhere. Your magnet is always primed for attraction. In this way, community is infinite, and opportunities for expansion are limitless.

Curiosities

*Where am I prioritizing relationship with
others over relationship with myself?
How can I genuinely connect with others?
Where am I manipulating others to earn their love and acceptance?*

Statements

*I own my emotions and allow them to flow freely.
I trust that all experiences have value.
I thrive in community because I belong within myself.*

EIGHT OF CLUBS

Intention in Your Knowing

Eight of Clubs energy can feel like riding the waves of universal knowledge; set your intention and drop in. When you let ideas, momentum, and communication flow, it is easeful to take inspired action. Inspiration will drop into your consciousness when you are in energetic flow. Yet you can't wait for inspiration to get into the flow. Inspiration is pointless without action.

Feeling like you need to know everything or be perfect at something before you have learned it can be isolating, leading you to quiet your voice and not express your truth. In this energy, you may resist ideas that come easily, questioning whether something is too good to be true. You may feel stubborn and want to dig your heels in, yet this is just another way to avoid moving forward. You are deepening a rut in which you feel comfortable . . . what happens when it's so deep you can't get out?

If the same old stories are rising up for resolution and you find yourself asking, *This again?* remind yourself that you can choose how to respond. If you intend for it to be different, then it will be.

This spark of self-awareness creates a clear connection to your intuition. It is in this connection where your knowing flows. Communication feels effortless, and you speak with clarity and confidence, knowing that others are receiving your message with the same energy.

If you are feeling in a rut, go out into the world and have experiences, meet people, and do things that will get your momentum going again. You have your unique way to get your energetic flow moving: What lights you up? Set your intention and go!

Curiosities

When do I own my ideas without forcing them on others; am I being strong-willed or stubborn?
What activity inspires me to get back into mental flow?
How can I connect into the universal flow of wisdom?

Statements

I can believe in myself without being a know-it-all.
I trust my intention and allow my intuition to flow through me.
I communicate my knowing with clarity and confidence.

EIGHT OF DIAMONDS

Intention in Values

Eight of Diamonds energy invites you to merge your inner and outer values. Put your money where your mouth is; there is no room for indecision. Don't question your intention, it is everything. Though this energy manifests physically, your internal values must match your intention for you to feel successful. Simply put: the grass is greener where you water it.

This energy is a magnet for abundance in the physical world, and yet oftentimes it is your insistence to control that is blocking the magnet and stopping the flow. If your internal value system and beliefs around money are not aligned with your actions in the outer world, you will leak money. Alignment will manifest more. Replace money with any other thing you value, and the concept remains the same.

In this energy, you have the opportunity to manifest, yet it can only be done through a deep understanding of yourself. Take responsibility for how you want to feel in the world. The Universe provides an abundance of opportunities; it is up to you to set your intention, be prepared, and then show up. What you feel inside is reflected outside—are you attracting or repelling what you say you want?

Eight of Diamonds energy can get stuck in a cycle of seeking external validation to justify your choice to control a situation. This limits your possibilities because you are only focusing on what you can see or on a specific result. Become intimate with your values. Trusting what feels good to you on the inside, not just what looks good to society on the outside, is the way to effectively channel this energy. Focus on your intended internal feeling and be open to how it manifests in the physical world. It might surprise you.

Curiosities

When are my intentions reflected in my physical world?
How can I be more confident in who I am, what
I value, and what feels good to me?
Where am I purposeful with my intentions?

Statements

When my alignment and intentions manifest
limitless possibilities, I take inspired action.
I am magnetic because I choose to focus on my intentions.
My focused intention creates expansion.

EIGHT OF SPADES

Intention in Transformation

Eight of Spades energy is about transformation and evolution within to experience flow and ease in life. As with any evolution, you can also get stuck in the past, toxic patterns, old ways of doing things, and resisting change.

This energy invites you to feel into your soul, the very core of who you are, and embody this energy to expand your essence. Imagine yourself as a lamp. You require power to light up the room. And yet you may be hesitant to embrace your power because you fear you won't have the capacity to channel the wattage. Rest assured that each time the current of power runs through you, it expands your capacity to hold more. You won't short-circuit, you'll simply shine brighter.

When you merge your inner being with your physical body, you ignite this personal power. This can manifest as success in all areas of life. It is a personal cycle of manifestation, a PhD in self. Your curriculum is not like anyone else's, which makes this journey lonely at times. And yet, when you commit to learning about what works best for you, you start to overcome things more rapidly and with seemingly less effort than imagined. You realize how far you have come and know it's time for even more expansion.

As your power increases, you must develop the capacity in your physical body to sustain it. This looks different for each person, and yet the common theme is to ensure it is not all or nothing. As you incorporate new habits and start to repeat practices, there is a point at which you must decide whether it's time to keep going or to switch things up. Are you ready to expand? At this decision point, it is imperative to be clear about your intention.

Sometimes you may get too set in your ways. *What's the harm?* you think. *It's always worked.* This is like planting the same seeds in the same area of your garden each year. Though you do get crops every year, your yield will diminish over time. You may feel hesitant to change what you're doing because it's worked in the past. And yet, what would happen if you were to do something differently? Expansion is possible if you intend for and nurture it.

If you're unsure of where to start, look for inspiration. Although you are independent, you don't need to do the work alone. Ask for help. Alone you have power; together we have impact.

Curiosities

*How can I fully embrace the discomfort of
my growth and transformation?
Where do I feel stagnant and isolated in life?
What practices do I need to integrate into my
life to support my overall well-being?*

Statements

*I know myself well enough to switch things up when necessary.
I am focused on my transformation and invested in a doctorate in me.
I am intentional in my desire to grow and am ready for more.*

NINE OF HEARTS

Releasing Expectations in Relationships

Nine of Hearts energy is letting go of how you *should* feel in relationships. This means accepting all aspects as they are and letting go of any expectations of how you, the other person, or the relationship itself *should* be. When you reflect on your relationship with self and see where your old ways, beliefs, and patterns are not serving you, this awareness begins your transformation.

Acceptance is objective. It just *is*. This energy specifically asks you to release any emotion you have tied to your expectations.

This energy can feel heavy, as though you are holding on to a form of relationship that you need to let go of and are resisting. You may feel this as desperation, resistance, or abandonment. When you release your expectations in relationships, you're releasing expectations and pressure you have on yourself, allowing for a feeling of liberation. When a relationship ends, society assumes there's been a massive conflict and wants to place blame on the guilty party. And yet oftentimes, the ending is simply because the relationship has run its course.

It can be hard to release old ideas and patterns because they feel nostalgic, like tradition. While you inherit traditions, you have a choice over whether you feel guilt or obligation to keep them. Traditions, after all, are only guidelines. There's no rule you have to send holiday cards each year just because your parents always did. Allow for the end of the old to be the beginning of the new.

Choosing doesn't necessarily mean a relationship needs to end. It could simply mean you need to release the dream or the expectation of how you thought the relationship would be and accept the present reality. Acceptance allows you to be more fully in the relationship rather than fantasize about it. Be in the now.

Curiosities

What expectations in relationships am I holding on to?
In releasing guilt and shame, what am I making room for?
What patterns do I see repeating?

Statements

When I accept things as they are, I free myself
from taking them personally.
The fewer "shoulds" I have in my backpack, the lighter I feel.
I know that releasing expectations allows for new possibilities.

NINE OF CLUBS

Releasing Expectations in Knowing

Nine of Clubs energy invites you to release ideas and thoughts that may seem antiquated. Get out the duster to clean the cobwebs and mental clutter from your mind. This creates space for your intuitive knowing, rather than analytical knowledge, and helps you communicate from a broader perspective.

Knowledge comes to you in all sorts of ways: through books, teachers, parents, friends, and observations of life. Yet there is also your inner knowing of your higher self. There is no one right way. Letting go of old thought patterns and old ways of how you *should* think—and the expectation that others *should* think the same as you—makes room for inspiration and fresh perspectives.

Your biggest source of knowledge is your higher self and connecting into your inner knowing. Nine of Clubs energy reminds you that in order to make room for your wisdom, you must create space for your intuition to be heard. Step into your own vast library of inner knowing and let go of your expectations. Here, you can listen to the whispers of your intuition. Trust that inner wisdom.

Are you allowing yourself to be a vessel for higher knowledge, releasing any expectation of how your intuition *should* feel? It doesn't have to be complicated to be true.

You've got a double dose of expectation because you are acutely aware of the potential of humanity. The busy noise in your head can cloud confidence, making it difficult to make decisions. Your mind is powerful; because of this you risk spending too much time there and ignoring how you feel. Remember, your heart is also powerful; allow it to work with your mind, not against it. When you do, you have a clear path forward.

When you are subjective, you are the gatekeeper to your intuition. You attempt to control it, judging when, where, and how to use it. When you are objective, you are the gateway for your intuition, trusting there is reason for the uncomfortable feelings that may arise. Stop trying to analyze your inner wisdom and simply accept it. You don't need to *understand* to *know*.

Curiosities

What old ideas or expectations am I holding on to?
What patterns become apparent when I ignore my intuition?
Where can I shift into a new belief system and let go of the "shoulds"?

Statements

I allow my intuition to be seen and heard without expectations.
I choose to think from a broader perspective.
I know I am more than my beliefs.

NINE OF DIAMONDS

Releasing Expectations in Your Values

Nine of Diamonds energy reflects your outward environment and your inward essence. It physically mirrors how you feel on the inside.

Your ability to release inaccurate reflections influences what shows up based on the values you hold. Letting go creates space for new possibilities. These releases can be tangible or intangible; most often, you need to get rid of expectations about the way things *should* be or how they are *supposed* to go. Let go of the potential of what *could* be and accept what is.

It's quitting the "dream job" once you realize it's no longer fulfilling. It's the help you hire to do those tasks that take up your valuable time. In these examples and many others, it's more than the thing you are letting go of. It's releasing the weight of expectations of yourself and others, and honoring how you feel on the inside. There is no need to justify your reasons, just do it.

Surrendering to what is and viewing your circumstances from a broader perspective creates space for your physical world to align with you. Nine of Diamonds energy may feel like a duality. The burden of conditions that you place on what you value leads to certain expectations of how things *should* be in your physical experience.

This physical energy wants to be seen and reflects what you are not seeing; it reflects what it is that you need to do. There is no need to prove your value through evidence in your physical environment. You are enough because you are. Period.

When you are subjective, you attach value to sentimental items. This is like connecting value to a memory that you feel might vanish if the physical thing no longer exists. When you are objective, you value the memory itself and trust that you don't need the physical reminder to prove it. It's like inheriting your great-grandma's fine tea set when you don't drink tea. Would you rather have it gather dust and take up space in your cupboard or give it to a home where it will be used? Take a picture of it, then release it. You don't have to keep it because it was given to you; just because your great-grandma treasured it, you don't have to. Instead, treasure the memories.

Curiosities

Where can I release the need for external validation?
Where is my value reflected in my life?
What opportunities am I not seeing because my vision is crowded?

Statements

My outer world reflects my inner world.
I am releasing expectations and allowing my self-worth to be reflected in my physical world.
I trust that I no longer need a physical reminder of a valuable experience.

NINE OF SPADES

Releasing Expectations in Transformation

Nine of Spades energy encourages you to release any expectations of how things *should* look, feel, or be when you are amid transformation. These transformations happen in many shapes and forms and on different timelines.

This energy wants you to give up the known for the unknown and applies to love, knowledge, values, purpose, and growth. It can feel hard, and there are no guarantees; yet what if . . . oh, the possibilities!

For example, as you sort through your wardrobe, you go down memory lane with each piece of clothing you are considering parting with. You may feel emotional and wonder whether you are done with this particular style, phase, or look. Are you ready to try something different? You contemplate these emotional decisions and consider whether you are ready to let go, donate, or sell your old clothes to make room for a new you.

When you are transforming and you understand your inner wisdom, you are on a journey of expansion to your full potential. When you are embodying your heart and mind and you see the infinite possibilities within yourself, you are transforming.

Nine of Spades energy asks you to release your subjective views and embrace a more objective unconditional perspective. It's not about you, although your mind will work hard to convince you that it is. Your soul understands impartiality and recognizes that it's your natural progression and part of your journey.

Just like in nature, loss is part of transformation. In fall, trees lose their leaves. And yet, we don't blame the tree. The tree is not dead, it is simply transforming. It's part of the cycle.

In this same way, don't blame yourself for wanting to transform. You are not supposed to wear the same clothes forever, you don't have to wear them until the thread is bare. Choose to release things when they no longer fit in your lifestyle. You are not expected to remain the same; life is a journey. Letting your expectations go liberates you to transform.

Curiosities

How do I step forward as the best version of myself?
What habits are getting in the way of my growth?
How am I showing up in my own personal transformation?

Statements

I honor my transformation.
I remove the weight of expectations and feel free.
I clear the way for my new intentions by releasing old patterns.

CHAPTER 8

Tens, Jacks, Queens, and Kings: Opportunity, Responsibility, Compassion, and Dedication

TEN OF HEARTS

Opportunity to Share in Relationships

Ten of Hearts energy offers you great success with groups of people. This is leadership energy, as long as you don't change yourself to please others.

This energy is attractive to others; you are a magnet. You get to choose who you spend time and energy with, who you attract, and who you repel. You feel confident in the awareness of what you've done and accomplished already.

It may feel easier to attract everything because you feel obligated or don't want to miss out, yet this leaves you feeling overwhelmed or lost in the crowd. Do you welcome only the opportunities that are right for you or take on everything that comes your way? Overwhelm happens when you accommodate other people's expectations and accept them as your own.

This energy requires connection with boundaries that inform what you choose to allow and accept. You cannot rely on anything external to you; it's up to you to discern when enough is enough. You have to be solid internally to capitalize on the abundance and potential of this energy.

At times you may feel as though the world owes you without you needing to exert any effort; however, the fullness of your potential and creativity is only available when you surrender to what is rather than what "should" be. Whether these expectations originate with you or with others, it's up to you to listen to your heart and soul as you choose and decide.

When you accept what is, you allow for blessings to shower on you. People seek you out, wanting to soak up your magnetism because the depth of your relationship with yourself and your worth is just oozing out of you. In the sea of opportunity, you get to choose whether you dull your shine to fit in *or* own it, belong, and lead. This is where your inner preparation meets outer opportunity.

Curiosities

Where am I feeling a sense of obligation in relationships?
When am I exercising discernment in choosing who I attract and repel?
How can I be more willing to let all aspects of me show?

Statements

I know I can lead and love at the same time.
I seize opportunities that are aligned for me.
I am willing to share my heart with more people.

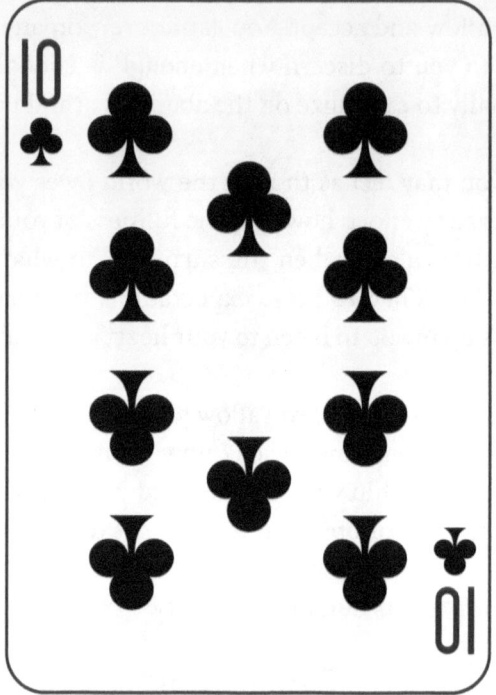

TEN OF CLUBS

Opportunity to Share Wisdom

Ten of Clubs energy offers you opportunities to share what you know. It carries the energy of mental accomplishment and independent thinking. You're able to bring many pieces of information together and form your own hypothesis. You're confident in your opinions, regardless of their popularity.

This energy demands freedom to do whatever you want whenever you choose. You may feel the need to convince people you're right and to justify your thoughts, even to yourself. Although you sometimes feel you know more than anyone else, remember that does not mean you do or that you are superior.

In this energy your head may feel so full that your mind is spinning round and round without making any progress; sometimes it may feel as though your mind has a life of its own and has taken over. It's time to reel your mind in, connect the dots, and reclaim your mental power. Realize you have power over your thoughts, choose which direction to focus on, and move forward.

Acquiring more knowledge only means your already-full head becomes even fuller. Why do you need to know it all? When you stop relying solely on your head so that you listen to your heart and intuition, and follow the guidance, you will step into vaster depths of knowledge and wisdom than you realized were possible. You get so caught up in the need to know it all, you overlook the wisdom to be found in riding with the current of your intuition. Rather than working harder and harder, if you'd pause—if you'd take time to zoom out and see the wood beyond the trees—you'd realize you're already there.

Stop collecting knowledge and go do something with it. You know it in theory, now go get practical. You already have all the puzzle pieces; it's time to put them together. You love variety and to have your finger in multiple pies at the same time; however, when you align with your heart and soul, you have unlimited potential. The golden opportunity is in choosing your focus over and over again so that you don't become distracted from what's truly important to you.

Curiosities

Where am I stuck in overthinking?
When am I trying to do it all when doing
less may well be more effective?
When am I open to receiving opportunities rather
than being overwhelmed by them?

Statements

I pause and choose where to focus my energy.
I accomplish enough when I am aligned and listening to my intuition.
I welcome aligned opportunities to share my knowledge.

TEN OF DIAMONDS

Opportunity to Share Value

Ten of Diamonds energy has every opportunity to receive abundantly and to succeed at anything you choose. In this energy you may be generous with others or possessive and materialistic. Which will you choose?

The key to this energy is to be aware of your blessings rather than feeling burdened by them. On the flip side, this energy can feel as if the whole world revolves around you and therefore owes you. Could it really be *this* easy?

This energy is confident, mirroring what's possible for others, especially when you're aligned and secure in your values. When you're aware of what you've accomplished, you see that opportunity is already all around you. If you focus on what you lack, you may miss or reject an opportunity that's right in front of you.

The diamond is the only symbol of the deck that looks the same whichever way you hold the card. Because of this, Ten of Diamonds energy may lead to you becoming entrenched in your view of the world. When you hold on to your views too tightly, you may dig in and refuse to budge, and limit the opportunities that are unfolding before you. Similar to when you overpack a suitcase, there's no room for anything new.

The strong magnetism of Ten of Diamonds energy can leave you feeling overwhelmed and obligated, because handling greater success requires being open to change so that you are able to expand your capacity for success. As a steward of giving and receiving energy, what will your next step be?

Even though you have oodles to share, you may be tempted to place expectations on others as a prerequisite to giving to them. Your lesson is to realize that not everyone holds the same values as you do and you have no right to coerce them or force your values on them as conditions.

You love to share generously with others. You reap what you sow, trusting that your unselfish intentions will be mirrored back to you. Remember, this is not all about you. You are a beautiful example of what is possible—not just for you, but for the world!

Curiosities

Do I owe the world or does the world owe me?
When do I feel lucky and yet not worthy?
How can I acknowledge my blessings every day?

Statements

As I see my success, I grow and expand who I am.
I recognize blessings in everyday life.
I am aware of opportunities to share my value.

TEN OF SPADES

Spiritual Opportunity

Ten of Spades energy delivers opportunities for you to deepen your spiritual connection. It encourages your focus to be more on the unseen than on the seen, and it wants you to pursue the mysteries of life.

As your spiritual connection becomes more prominent in your life, and fulfilling your purpose doesn't feel like work, you may feel less attached to the material world. When you choose to stay attached to the material world, and focus only on what you can see, you may feel obligated to work harder to justify the opportunities you receive because you neglect the unseen.

When this energy is present in your life, you get to choose whether you perceive what you receive as a blessing or an obligation. What are you going to do with your immense intuitive wisdom? You don't need that doctorate; the wisdom you already have is enough, and it's time to share it purposefully.

Ten of Spades energy can show up as you checking out energetically while still going through the motions—even though you remain in a situation, working hard to keep going on as even a keel as possible. You may feel in-between, as though you've outgrown your past self yet don't quite fit into your new self. While it is tempting to continue working hard to hang on to what was, the reality is that you can no longer be who you were without feeling underwhelmed and unsatisfied, swirling in the unknown. Deep transformation occurs when you're willing to make no-man's-land your home, to be you. Even when you feel as though you are a vast untamed wilderness, realize that *you* are the home *you* seek. Give yourself permission to own your freedom to be *you*.

The lesson in Ten of Spades energy is realizing your home—your spiritual and energetic home—is you. As you deepen your connection with spirit and self, you may find superficial relationships are replaced by deep, more meaningful ones. You are free to walk your own path without allowing outside influences to taint your journey.

Curiosities

How can I allow myself to move deeper into the unseen?
How can I be more spiritually connected and aware?
What am I willing to do with all the opportunities I have?

Statements

When I deepen my awareness of the unseen, I
unlock opportunities with ease and grace.
I know I am always energetically supported by the unseen.
As my spiritual connection strengthens, I become a more
powerful mirror of what's possible for others.

JACK OF HEARTS

Responsibility in Relationships

Jack of Hearts energy invites you to play and experiment with how you feel in relationships, to choose what's important for you over what's expected by others.

As you evolve, there's an ongoing need for you to realign in relationships. This energy reminds you that when you allow your mind to trust your heart, you give yourself permission to honor your own feelings. This provides space for your relationships to expand and flourish. Jack of Hearts energy asks you to trust your feelings, and to believe in yourself and your role in relationships. Being willing to not judge yourself is important in this energy; all your feelings and experiences are valid.

Notice that on the card itself, the feather and the ax indicate the dilemma of this energy in relationships. Jack of Hearts energy can be the proverbial martyr who sacrifices for love and for others. Giving the whole pie away is not the answer; neither is keeping it all, even if that's what you really, really want. Honoring your feelings requires you to have boundaries and discernment. Be gentle and firm with yourself, as you would a child.

You can choose your own heart even when it's not what's expected by other people. This could look like choosing love over family responsibility—for example, a third-generation farmer choosing not to take over the family farm. The lesson in this energy is to learn appropriate responsibility in relationships, creating win-win scenarios that are mutually beneficial. Through these lessons, you access deeper levels of love and spiritual awareness.

This energy is learned through feelings and heartbreak; you have to feel it to move through it. If you've had your heart broken—congratulations. Be a heartbreak specialist!

Trust that each time your heart is brave enough to try again, you are more confident in accepting and expressing your feelings. Living on your own terms is about choosing them, not accepting them from others. Embrace the power of choosing your own heart, and watch relationships unfold.

Curiosities

When am I owning and honoring my feelings?
Where is my boundary between serving and sacrificing?
How can I choose my own terms and respect
others in my relationships?

Statements

I can fully love someone else without sacrificing myself.
I allow my heart to learn the lessons, even when it feels scary.
I know that serving and loving others requires loving myself first.

JACK OF CLUBS

Responsibility in Communication

Jack of Clubs energy wants you to be grounded in self-concept so you can communicate your thoughts and concepts wisely and responsibly. You may be viewed as a visionary or you may come across as a know-it-all; the difference is in whether you're exercising reasonable responsibility.

This energy encourages you to be expansive, creative, and curious, remembering who you are and how you communicate your thoughts and concepts as you serve others through your creativity. Imagine you're the poet on the street corner, youthful yet wise beyond your years. Be willing to learn from various sources other than formal educators. Be willing to share in a variety of ways, rather than limiting yourself to expected traditions.

You see what's possible and believe you know best. You may become tempted to criticize because you see all flaws and can become impatient of yourself and others. The self-important story you spin in your head becomes your reality, leading you to feel the need to police others.

In this energy, you want so much to be heard that, when you feel misunderstood, you become more forceful in your oration or repeat yourself over and over. When you become responsible in your communication, you are able to say what you mean in a way that everyone can understand.

Jack of Clubs energy can spin a good story that may or may not be true and correct. Spinning a story shows creativity and imagination, yet it can also be used with ill intent to manipulate or deceive. Are you pulling the wool over your own eyes or those of others? You can be such a good storyteller that you can create beliefs that aren't true.

Notice that on the card itself, the Jack of Clubs' face and feather convey mischief and playfulness; wide-open eyes indicate an openness to learn and a readiness to absorb new knowledge and wisdom. Do you mean to control or inspire?

You feel safe when you are deeply connected to your soul and rely on your intuition to guide and direct your growth and transformation. Without that connection you may play the field, seeking to be in the "in" crowd. You are the storyteller and are meant to connect through sharing your story with others, as well as hold space as a curator for theirs.

Curiosities

When am I exaggerating to appear or feel more confident?
Where am I placing too much responsibility on sharing all I know?
How can I best serve others through my creativity and knowledge?

Statements

I view the role of teacher and student as equal partners.
My only responsibility is to understand and inspire myself.
I know the power my message has for others, so
I choose to communicate responsibly.

J♣

JACK OF DIAMONDS

Responsibility in Value

Jack of Diamonds energy carries strong persuasive power. When aligned with your values, tangible success is assured in this energy—even though it may not necessarily be easy. When not aligned, you may feel the need to prove your value through external validation.

This energy is willing to show up persistently, to keep knocking, to do whatever it takes because you believe deeply in the value you offer. Become a rejection specialist, taking each no as fuel for the next opportunity. Are you pleasantly surprised or skeptical that it could really be that easy?

Jack of Diamonds energy is smart, witty, and charming, possessing great skills of persuasion. It is creative, social, and entertaining. In this energy, you believe you can do anything, especially when others tell you that you can't. What if it all works out? Can you trust yourself and ignore the naysayers?

Notice that on the card itself, the Jack of Diamonds' eyes are on the prize, gaze firmly fixed on the diamond. You are aware of what is important and prominent in your world; trust your value system, be bold, and take that leap of faith in sharing your value with the world. You have the potential to vigorously protect what you believe is yours.

This energy is willing to push boundaries, to play and experiment with different ways of serving others. It keeps on trying to discover what works and what doesn't. Jack of Diamonds energy is willing to walk the line. Yet when you cross it, you may be tempted to make shady deals, to give up your integrity to get what you want.

The moment you take this energy seriously, you lose the lightness and overthink it. Playfulness is required to reap the rewards of this energy. Reach for more—because why not? You may get it! Have fun bending the rules responsibly. Are you seeking permission or are you content with forgiveness?

Your powerful magnetism requires you to create a strong foundation for your success and popularity. To be sustainable, you need to dig below the surface and allow your sixth sense to play.

Curiosities

*Where am I putting my own gain above the
needs of those I am here to serve?
Where am I attached to the outcome of my actions?
How can I be willing to learn as much from my
failures as I do from my successes?*

Statements

*I am willing to share value with others and be
unattached to how they choose to respond.
I am honest and up front in my dealings with others.
I contribute responsibly, in integrity with my values.*

JACK OF SPADES

Spiritual Responsibility

Jack of Spades energy asks you to focus on your inner growth. This can feel like work or purpose depending on how you approach it. The role of this energy is to serve with spiritual purpose and help others become familiar with the unseen. There is always more for you to discover and uncover. Rather than feeling daunted, you're excited. What's next?

This energy embodies confidence; it trusts the unseen. Never satisfied, Jack of Spades knows that there's always something more. You're keen to move forward with trust, confidence, excitement, and anticipation, to get to what's next rather than making space to acknowledge the progress you've made and the wisdom you've acquired thus far.

This energy could show up as cocky rather than confident. As the debutante being presented at the ball, you believe you've made it, that you're a fully fledged adult, yet this is only the beginning of deeper learning. Are you willing to take responsibility, or do you just want to play dress-up?

The ongoing work of this energy is to be in integrity and get out of your head. It's time to put those stacks of self-help books back on the shelf, and actually do the work. Jack of Spades energy comes with a responsibility to stay humble and resist the temptation to expect too much from others. To be effective, Jack of Spades energy reminds you of the importance of being aligned in all facets of life and of the ongoing requirement to realign as you grow and evolve.

Notice that on the card, we see only one of this Jack's eyes because this energy is focused on inner work. This Jack holds up a mirror to be aware of the need to keep on growing and transforming. The youthful enthusiasm of Jack of Spades energy is a gift when paired with deeper inner responsibility for your own spiritual transformation and potential.

You can step into leadership with humility and be ready to learn, *or* you can lazily lie back and be overconfident in what you already know. Remain curious and keep going; transformation is never-ending. Everyone transforms at their own pace and in their own way. Your path, your pace.

Curiosities

How can I align my actions with what I say?
Where am I focusing too much on my own
needs rather than serving others?
How can I support and encourage others on their inner growth
and spiritual journey while staying on my own path?

Statements

I am responsible for being aligned and on purpose.
I serve others in a way that exemplifies my deep spiritual connection.
I embody authenticity with humility.

QUEEN OF HEARTS

Compassion in Relationship

Queen of Hearts energy is traditionally seen as the embodiment of nurturing, motherly love. It is kind, encouraging, and supported by loving boundaries.

When you've ignored nurturing yourself and you're pouring from an empty cup, you may become oversacrificing, judgmental, and harsh. The solution is to always love, appreciate, and honor yourself first. In times when you are struggling, this may mean you put your oxygen mask on first and take a breath before helping others. In times of flourishing, you still keep filling your own cup first so you can love others more effectively from your overflow.

When your cup is full of charm and grace, you are able to win over any room you enter. Assured and confident, Queen of Hearts energy is more concerned with the beauty of emotions and the influence you have on the world than with your own outward beauty.

Just as you're required to set loving boundaries with others, you're also required to set loving boundaries with yourself. Beware of crossing into overindulgence to fill the void, a place that *feels* empty inside of you. This void is meant to be present in all of us, and if you try to fill it with external things, you miss your potential. Being comfortable with the void and having the ability to feel your feelings is what propels your growth.

Imagine a mother who does absolutely everything to ensure her child avoids any uncomfortable feelings. This is exhausting and unsustainable for the mother, and it also inhibits the child's growth and development. The key here is holding the void rather than filling it.

When you are connected to your soul and aligned, you feel valued and appreciated rather than obligated and isolated. Your power and potential are in deepening your relationship with your soul rather than seeking superficial rewards.

Queen of Hearts energy shows that love can reveal who you are, how you show up, and how you relate to others. Kindness is a choice. Love is a decision. Compassion is always the answer.

Curiosities

*Where would my relationships benefit from me
establishing considerate boundaries?
When am I kind, caring, and benevolent without strings attached?
How can I foster more compassion for myself?*

Statements

*I feel safe in the void.
Love is an action.
How I show up creates my experience.*

QUEEN OF CLUBS

Compassion in the Knowing

Queen of Clubs energy brings the gift of knowledge, creativity, and resourcefulness, with a deep desire to succeed in whatever endeavor you choose to pursue. This energy is nurturing and committed to service through sharing wisdom.

As the mother of intuition, you have the maturity to embrace intuitive energy and the unseen. You're also committed to sharing that information with those who are ready to receive it. Yet knowing when and where to share is key. Remember: conflict is more likely than acceptance when you offer unsolicited advice. The boundary with yourself is most important here, knowing when to offer advice, when to listen, and when to appreciate the nuance of permission. Trust yourself to read the room.

Queen of Clubs energy has a certain stature that doesn't take direction from others easily. Driven and determined, this energy can be dictatorial, impatient, and intolerant: *you should believe this because I do; you have to agree with me.* You possess a powerful mind and strong will, yet you must wield your power carefully. When Queen of Clubs energy gets stuck in a loop of overthinking, you may become bossy or pushy, punishing others who don't see things your way. Coercion doesn't benefit anyone.

Even when they do ask your opinion, other people might not always heed your wise advice. It can be easy to take this personally, or you may even doubt your intuition. The invitation is simply to trust. Others make their own decisions and mistakes, just as you do.

You are wise beyond your years, and the channel for divine guidance flowing through you is unmatched. Some things are better left unsaid, though, and it's up to you to discern the difference. Just because you don't say something doesn't mean it's not important. Your value is in your *knowing* rather than others *needing your knowing*. It's never your wisdom that's the problem; it's who you share it with as well as how, when, and why.

When your sense of self is strong and you leave your *shoulds* outside the door, you are able to trust yourself without worrying about what might or might not happen.

Queen of Clubs energy reminds you to incorporate heart and soul as well as your mind, consistently relying on your intuition. This energy reinforces that communication with your higher self is vital for you to feel empowered. Listen to understand rather than to respond.

Curiosities

When am I trusting my intuition rather than getting lost in my head?
How are my heart, soul, and mind in agreement?
How can I share my wisdom intentionally and compassionately?

Statements

*I know that my thoughts are mine and I have
no right to enforce them on others.
I choose to nurture with patience and pure intention.
I am guided by my knowing.*

QUEEN OF DIAMONDS

Compassion in Values

Queen of Diamonds energy requires you to be rooted in your values with an open heart and mind, so you can pollinate and expand your gifts into the world. You see each person as a unique flower and notice the value in everything and everyone. Trust that a flower needs a bee to pollinate it.

You may be tempted to dwell too much on looks and material accomplishments. The importance of realizing everything you have to offer—not just physical things—is the way you expand your value. Without a firm foundation to your belief system, without knowing what's really important, this energy can fall into the trap of seeking external validation rather than giving from abundance. Compassion reminds you of where your values lie.

Without compassion, this energy falls into doing everything from ego, for money, or for self-centered reasons. Giving without conditions is your key to expanding what's possible and to trusting your own growth and transformation as you journey along your path.

In this energy, you can get lost in doing too much for others. If you overgive time and resources, even to good causes, you are not honoring yourself. Stay grounded in your value system. Contributions come in many forms and are just one aspect of your worth. You are more than the things you do and give; you are more than the sum of your actions. So there is no need to try to balance the equation. Be the queen of delegation: wise enough to allow people's strengths to shine.

As the Queen of Diamonds, you must invest in yourself. Trust that every investment you make in others is valuable even when the results you expect don't eventuate. You cannot control the performance of your investments, you can only control the energy with which you invest. When you are strong in your own values, this energy can give and give. As long as you're connected into yourself, you won't waver. Invest in yourself. Your energy is your greatest contribution to the world—the return will be worth it.

Curiosities

How can I be generous from my heart or my head?
How can I be aware when I step out of integrity in my values?
Where am I investing in myself?

Statements

I invest in what's important to me and encourage
others to invest in what's important to them.
My compassion and trust for others nurtures and expands their value.
I am more than enough without seeking external validation.

QUEEN OF SPADES

Spiritual Compassion

Queen of Spades energy is a born leader, with an innate ability to shine in any situation. This energy wants to be rather than do. You may exude confidence in your transformation and expansion, certain in your awareness of the unseen and its influence, and yet this confidence and certainty may feel like a burden.

While all the other Queens are looking at the suit emblem on the card, the Queen of Spades is looking in the other direction. You are not looking at worldly objects—your mind is in other places. Your understanding is complete, your boundaries are in place, and your inner wisdom is here to help you with pure intention.

You can study books all you want, yet there comes a moment when you realize your gut instinct knew what to do, with unwavering stability, all along. And in this moment, you decide to trust yourself over the tested information. A recent graduate does something differently on the job than they were taught in school. A new mom abandons all the how-to books in favor of following her own inner wisdom. A gardener snips off the branch that's not growing as vitally as the rest instead of digging the bush out completely. Growth isn't always visible or easy to quantify.

Notice that on the card, this Queen holds a scepter as a symbol of potential power and deep spiritual strength to remind you that using your power is a choice rather than an obligation. You know you are ready for whatever the world sends your way, and yet sometimes this causes you to take on too much; this may lead to overworking and overdelivering.

In this energy, there may be pivotal moments when crucial changes are destined to occur; you may wonder whether your spiritual awareness is a gift or a burden. In these moments, find stillness to access your prowess. Your innate power comes from your experience rather than what you've learned. Within your spiritual connection you find wisdom. It is through being in the unseen that you find yourself.

Curiosities

*How can I show compassion for others in their transformation
while allowing space for them to be in their journey?
Where are my boundaries when nurturing
others in their spiritual growth?
When am I seeing my awareness as a gift rather than an obligation?*

Statements

*I embrace unquantifiable growth.
I know I have what it takes to handle any situation that comes my way.
I shift and change as led by my inner wisdom
even when I can't see the outcome.*

Q
♠

KING OF HEARTS

Dedication in Relationship

King of Hearts energy reminds you that love is the foundation for everything. This energy wants everyone to be soaked in a container of love in a benevolent, fatherly kind of way. The full power of this energy cannot be accessed without you knowing and owning your own worth.

In this energy, you love others from the overflow of you loving yourself; love from this place rather than from the fumes of your self-denial. The deeper your self-worth is, the more love you have to give without draining yourself.

You radiate an energy that expands your ability to accept and give support to others. King of Hearts energy leads by example: love yourself and love others so they can do the same. Imagine a king knighting a member of the court. As they face each other, the king says, *I see this quality in you. Do you see it in you?* It is only when the recipient acknowledges and accepts the king's words and support that they truly embody the role as a knight.

This emotional confidence prioritizes truth and fairness in all interactions, and yet has potential to be aggressive, demanding, and controlling in relationships.

Notice that on the card, there are multiple hearts on the robe, which serve as a literal reminder for you to wear your heart on your sleeve. When you feel safe in yourself, you are more able to be vulnerable in your emotions and you're able to accept your own emotions. You have the potential to be a container of emotional safety for yourself and for others.

Unlike the other Kings, both of the King of Hearts' hands are visible, which indicates a willingness to do whatever it takes to support others. Your strength comes through being willing to ask for help when required. Through vulnerability comes the courage to lead.

The sword is raised up, ready to protect those in the realm, to stand up for what's right, and to defend against opponents. Stand firm and own your feelings. Kingly leadership requires emotional honesty.

Curiosities

How do I support and lead with emotional honesty?
When do my actions affect others in relationships?
How can I help others see in themselves what I know to be true?

Statements

I am dedicated to leading by example.
I am willing to be vulnerable and ask for help.
I choose to use my emotional strength for the benefit of all involved in the situation.

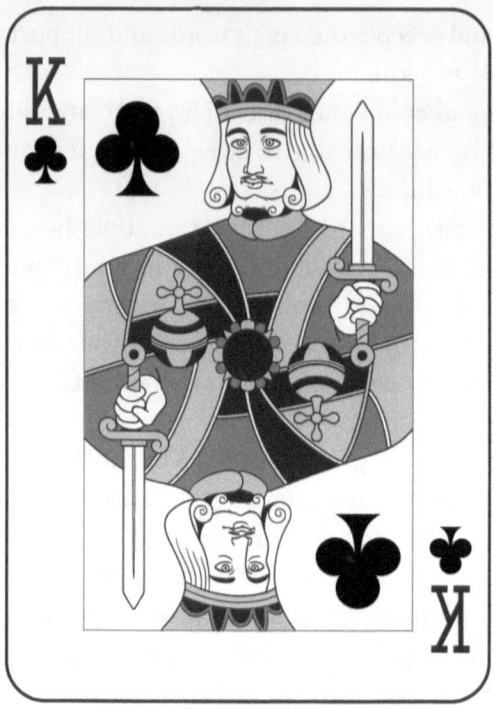

KING OF CLUBS

Dedication in Wisdom

King of Clubs energy is more dedicated to wisdom than anything else. You lead the way with creative insights and are always open to learning.

This energy, while embodying dexterity of mind, values calm and collected wisdom over a busy, frenetic brain. The best innovation and creative solutions come from the absence of thought. Imagine the power of clearing your mind with meditation, a walk in the woods, or a long, hot shower. Ideas are cultivated in the space between intuition and creativity.

As a thought leader, you demonstrate confidence in your intuition, wisdom, creativity, ideas, and communication. You are a subject matter expert, and yet you realize you don't know everything. This can be a vulnerable space. At times, you can be overly authoritative to protect your insecurity about perceived gaps in your knowledge. It is important to be confident enough in who you are to know there is always room for growth.

You're creative and playful in coming up with new ways to share your wisdom with others, yet you may fall prey to believing you have to do it in the accustomed ways. Break out of the box and lead in your own way.

You have so much wisdom and are deeply dedicated to sharing it with others compassionately so they acknowledge and appreciate their own wisdom. Your thirst for deeper wisdom is led by your intuition because you know you can't do it alone.

You don't have to behave like a know-it-all to be all-knowing. Intelligence is knowing when to pick up the mic and when to keep your mouth shut. Use your knowledge as a tool rather than a weapon. As a lifelong learner, you realize your wisdom does not come from outside sources. You are the wisdom you seek.

Curiosities

When am I confident in myself to defend my truth respectfully?
How willing am I to keep my mouth shut even
when I have a contrary opinion?
Where am I modeling leading with others
rather than wanting to dominate?

Statements

I use my knowledge and wisdom to help others see their own greatness.
My mind is organized, logical, wise, and intuitive.
I am dedicated to deepening my inner wisdom.

K♣

KING OF DIAMONDS

Dedication in Value

King of Diamonds energy asks you to be confident that wealth can come easily; living in integrity ensures that monetary success will be provided. This energy understands the value in all forms of currency and reminds you that all that glitters is not gold. It also encourages you to understand your worth and step in a little more, even just a baby step. King of Diamonds energy reminds you to value yourself and your services so that others understand the value as well.

Even though this energy expands your possibility for abundance, wealth, and success, your intention can never be how to get ahead monetarily. When your eye is on the prize, that tunnel vision can make you ruthless and manipulative. Focus on embodying your values to avoid showing up as money-hungry or materialistic. Traditionally, one of the King's hands is extended into a greeting or handshake, while the other is hidden behind his back. This indicates the temptation of this energy to engage in shady deals to get ahead.

Notice that on the card, there are a lot of diamonds. This reminds you to play with abundance and wealth and always be in alignment with your value and self-worth. Seize opportunities that come your way, and mirror the evolution of your values in everything you do. Remain in integrity, trust your value system, and be pure in your intentions.

Lead by doing rather than dictating how others *should* do something. The more you evolve and embody your value, the more others can see their value as well. When you model valuing yourself and what you do, you open the possibility for others to understand their own value and potential. You are reminded to be dedicated to your own judgment of what's important in life. Trust your value system and be pure in your intentions.

You know that actions without heart have no merit, so you bring love into all you do. You are the portrait of possibilities.

Curiosities

What is really important in my physical experience?
Where might I be manipulating situations in an attempt to hinder others from winning in case it means I lose?
How can I acknowledge that my return on investment may be something other than monetary?

Statements

I know that someone else's success is not my failure.
I am dedicated to being a consistent and trustworthy role model.
I am willing to allow others to see what I value.

K
♦

KING OF SPADES

Spiritual Dedication

King of Spades energy is magnetic. You can readily feel it, yet it can't be seen—you just have to trust. This energy blends the practical and the unseen, weaving it all together. As the artisan of the unseen with prowess in transformation, King of Spades energy is the secret sauce that makes all the elements of the dish come together.

When this energy focuses on the seen, you may feel a false sense of being superior to others; this is a reminder to lean into your spiritual connection.

In this energy you have the advantage and disadvantage of the bird's-eye view. You can see everything: allow yourself to be the role model of all role models and pave the path, trusting that whoever is ready will follow. Seeing the whole scope of things can also be a burden because you may want to control everything. Yet when you leave your perch to nitpick the details, you lose sight of the whole picture.

The King of Spades is a powerful and effective leader, showing you where to look rather than telling you the answer. Incredible wisdom is shared through a poem, song lyrics, or story—like a guide, gently nudging you along. Yet, this energy can at times forget the difference between the seen and the unseen, seek to control others, and become annoyed with those who are not spiritually aware. Defend your spiritual connection each time you find yourself at another growth edge. Trust that where you're being guided to is where you're meant to be.

You have the image in your mind of what you want to create—and what's more, you have the power to create it! It takes dedication; you can only add one ingredient at a time. In order to move more quickly, you may feel tempted to seek instructions from outside sources. Yet, why would you when you are able to create your own unique recipe? It's like you have the taste in your mouth of what you want for dinner: Will you spend hours searching for the recipe rather than realizing *you* are the perfect ingredient and have everything you need to create your vision as you go, one ingredient at a time?

Your journey is yours alone, and your transformation is invisible to the human eye. There's no need to measure progress according to anyone else's standard. There is no scorecard in life, and you're never behind or in front when you're on your own path.

Curiosities

Where could I connect more to my higher, wise self?
How can I remain grounded and spiritually connected?
Where can I use my power more wisely as led by spirit?

Statements

I live spiritually connected.
I model spiritual dedication because I own my path.
I deepen my spiritual dedication as I weave the seen and unseen.

CHAPTER 9

Joker: Infinite Possibilities

THE JOKER

Infinite Possibilities

Friend or foe? The Joker can be either, both, or neither. You get to choose because this card can emulate any card energy it wants. In every deck of cards, the Joker presents differently. Yet, you will most likely see all four suit emblems present, even if they are hidden. Look closely!

Historically, the Joker was the court jester, who ascended the throne on Fools' Day each year and impersonated the king, queen, jack, and all members of the kingdom. In doing so, the Joker showed everyone how to lighten up a little and not take life so seriously.

This energy can have you confused one moment and full of hope and laughing the next. The Joker ushers in a playful energy, bridging the gap between love and transformation. Truly an energy of infinite possibilities, it is a disco ball that never stops spinning.

The Joker card represents zero in the deck, which is a symbol of infinite possibilities. This can feel expansive and yet also overwhelming. Imagine going into an ice-cream shop with one hundred flavors and having to pick one. Where do you even begin? Sometimes the more you taste-test, the less sure you are. Your palate just becomes more and more confused and indecisive when faced with too many choices. When you realize that there is no right choice, that it's all about experimentation, you can play and have fun again.

The Joker impersonates others as an energetic chameleon. So, who are you? When faced with insecurity, you may wonder where you belong and use humor to deflect your lack of self-awareness. You may feel rudderless or like you are navigating without a map. Your path is within you. The challenge is to accept who you are.

This energy is playful, creative, independent, and not fond of being told what to do. Others may sometimes underestimate you because you love to play, yet you're not trying to teach, mother, or even lead others—you're simply reflecting back to them what is possible. This energy runs deeper than you may realize; do not underestimate your potential. Yes, life truly can be this much fun! You are the unconscious spark that ignites creative possibility.

Curiosities

If I knew there wasn't a right choice, what would I choose?
If anything were possible, who would I be?
What's holding me back or propelling me forward?
Why not?

Statements

I respect the value of playful experimentation.
I playfully navigate without a map.
I dream big because I trust that the possibilities are infinite.
I create my own path.

GLOSSARY

As authors, we intentionally chose specific words to describe the energetic concepts we have conveyed. In a world where there are many perspectives, we recognize that there is no universal definition for these terms. Therefore, we created this glossary to help you understand the particular context of the language we chose and to introduce you to other related terms.

Alignment: A position of agreement or alliance; when your mind, body, heart, and spirit are in agreement at a specific moment in time.
Appropriate: Fitting, suitable, purposeful.
Attachment: A deep and enduring emotional bond, an energetic tie.
Awareness: The knowledge and understanding that something is happening or exists.
Balance: Harmony in the parts of a whole.
Birth Card: The card in the Sun position on your date of birth, representing your life's contract.
Choice: The act of selecting your desired intention based on values and beliefs; can happen consciously or unconsciously.
Compassion: Trust, care, and support given with an open and kind heart in an effort to alleviate discomfort.
Consciousness: State of awareness of yourself and your surroundings.
Core values: Fundamental principles that guide your decisions and actions; they reflect what is important to you or what is central to your purpose or identity.
Decision: A commitment to the choices you make or don't make.
Desire: A feeling of wanting or wishing for something, driven by personal preferences.

Growth: The unseen process of expansion beyond your current state of being.

Higher self: Your soul that goes with you through many lifetimes, unencumbered by ego.

Holding space: The ability to be fully present and able to create a safe, nonjudgmental environment in which to feel, explore, and process emotions; can be for the self or others.

Intention: The energy behind your actions.

Intuition: Instinctive understanding without any need for justification or conscious reasoning.

Karma: Following as effect from cause.

Karmic influences: An energetic guardrail that provides a reminder that your choices have consequences.

Knowing: A feeling in the heart rather than intellectual knowledge.

Magick: Energy of the Universe that allows you to create through the direction and power of your intention, moving you closer to fulfilling your most authentic path in life.

Mindfulness: The act of purposefully bringing your attention to the present moment in order to cultivate awareness, without judging or reacting.

Mirror: The reflection of your sense of self.

Needs: Desires that your mind decided were necessities or requirements for well-being.

Nonattachment: The ability to not hold emotional bonds or energetic ties.

Ownership: The ability to accept a situation, outcome, or event.

Purpose: Intentionality in creation; the reason you exist on Earth.

Role model: Someone who serves as an example or inspiration, often looked up to as a guide.

Seen: Something that is tangible, material, and quantifiable.

Seer: An individual who accesses information through all senses.

Self-development: The process of learning new things and building new skills.

Shadow side: The feeling of unease in the process of growth.

Shadow work: The process of uncovering and getting to know parts of yourself that you are not consciously aware of.

Solar Value: The numerological value attributed to each card.

Soul agreement: A connection between souls decided upon before birth.
Spiritual: Relating to the spirit or soul; those intangible aspects of our existence that go beyond the physical body or material world.
Spot Value: The number of spots of a card, irrespective of suit.
Suit Value: The numerological influence specific to each suit.
Transformation: A profound personal shift or evolution.
Universal energy: The life force that exists all around and is felt by all living beings.
Unseen: Something that is unable to be physically seen or quantified.
Unseen world: The nontangible, energetic environment beyond the scope of ordinary perception, such as your intuition, inner knowing, or feelings; sometimes described as your sixth sense.

ADDITIONAL INFORMATION

You can find additional information on the history of the system and how to use it on our website at 8ofdiamondscollective.com.

CALCULATION FOR BIRTH CARD

Each day of the year has an underlying numerical value, called a solar value. This is different than the spot value on the card (where, e.g., Ace is 1 and King is 13).

> Suit value (the emblem value): Hearts = 0, Clubs = 13, Diamonds = 26, and Spades = 39

Then, you add spot to the suit to get the solar value.

The other way to calculate this is:

Day + 2(Month) = A
55 – A = Solar Value

For example, November 18:

18 + 2(11) = 40
55 – 40 = 15

The solar value for November 18 is 15, which is Two of Clubs.

Solar Values

Joker	0						
A♥	1	A♣	14	A♦	27	A♠	40
2♥	2	2♣	15	2♦	28	2♠	41
3♥	3	3♣	16	3♦	29	3♠	42
4♥	4	4♣	17	4♦	30	4♠	43
5♥	5	5♣	18	5♦	31	5♠	44
6♥	6	6♣	19	6♦	32	6♠	45
7♥	7	7♣	20	7♦	33	7♠	46
8♥	8	8♣	21	8♦	34	8♠	47
9♥	9	9♣	22	9♦	35	9♠	48
10♥	10	10♣	23	10♦	36	10♠	49
J♥	11	J♣	24	J♦	37	J♠	50
Q♥	12	Q♣	25	Q♦	38	Q♠	51
K♥	13	K♣	26	K♦	39	K♠	52

ACKNOWLEDGMENTS

DAPHNE

My heart is full of gratitude for Beth, Karen, and Jessica, and for our journey together. I appreciate my younger self, whose journey through the years has shaped me into the woman I've become. I am who I am today because of my four children. I'm grateful for the many, many clients I've worked with over the years who have been a large part of my growth and transformation journey. And I'm deeply appreciative of you, the reader, for choosing our book to discover the magick in you.

KAREN

With immense gratitude, I extend my heartfelt thanks to those who have played pivotal roles in bringing this project to life.

To my beloved children, Ashley and Noah: Your unwavering encouragement, support, and understanding have been the pillars that sustained me through countless hours of writing, creative research trips, and moments of sacrifice. Your selflessness allowed this project to move forward, and I'm profoundly grateful for your love.

To my coauthors, Daphne, Jessica, and Beth: A special acknowledgment to the incredible women who collaborated with me on this transformative journey. Your patience with my myriad of stories, our intuitive wisdom combined, and your unwavering commitment have been the cornerstone of this collaborative endeavor. Together, we translated countless narratives into words infused with energy. I've felt a unique trust and commitment from the beginning, and my heart, mind, and soul have blossomed through this shared experience. This collaboration feels like a reunion of souls, walking a path many lifetimes in the making. We've birthed this book that was conceived ages ago, and I'm profoundly grateful for this journey.

As we celebrate the fruition of what was once just a spark of an idea, I also extend my deepest thanks to each of you reading this book. May the energy within these pages resonate with the world, carrying the essence of our collective vision to all who are open to receiving it.

BETH

I am forever grateful to my three coauthors for teaching me the art of respect and genuine cooperation. To my husband for never making fun of me when I talk about spirits and numerological patterns; my children for teaching me love and patience; and my family and friends who have supported my spiritual untucking while I've "run their numbers" and tapped into their energetic space! I also appreciate you, as the reader, for having an open mind and heart to unlock the *amazingness* of your human journey.

JESSICA

I want to express my deepest gratitude to all the incredible souls who have supported me on this journey. Your unwavering belief in me and this work has been a constant source of inspiration. I want to thank my younger self, an integral part of the book's creation. Special appreciation goes to Beth, Daphne, and Karen for their contributions to my growth, learning, and healing. I want to thank my husband and two children for keeping me grounded and never letting me forget my true purpose in life is simply being me. Lastly, I want to acknowledge and appreciate you, the reader, who, with curiosity and vulnerability, is embarking on a journey to discover your true self alongside us. Here's to embracing our true purpose and living our best lives!

ABOUT THE AUTHORS

DAPHNE WELLS sees what others don't and uses her vision to revolutionize the way women do business. As the numerologist for leaders, she makes it easy for overextended women in business to turn overwhelm and self-doubt into self-mastery and extraordinary leadership. When she's not *inspiriting* women around the globe to rewrite the rules of business leadership, you'll find Daphne creating magick with fabric and threads, getting her hands dirty growing what she eats, or frolicking in the waves near her home in the beautiful South Island of New Zealand.

As an Ace of Clubs, Daphne embraces who she is as an idea machine. After decades of business leadership, she knew she needed to figure out a new way of being that didn't involve sacrificing herself for others and continuing the cycle of repeated adrenal fatigue and burnout.

Daphne believes we all have a built-in drive to be who we are coded to be—regardless of who anyone else wants us to be—and the battle between these two desires is essential in our growth.

Find her online at daphnewells.com.

Author Photo © Alan Dove

ABOUT THE AUTHORS

KAREN SMALL, a Canadian West Coast resident, is a multifaceted soul whose life revolves around creativity, exploration, and self-discovery. As a numerologist, EFT practitioner, writer, and creative, Karen delves deep into the human experience to unveil the patterns and connections that shape our lives.

As a Three of Clubs, Karen has always had a passion for understanding people's stories and sharing her own. Her journey took a transformative turn in 2017 during a midlife awakening, leading her to embrace numerology as a guiding force. This inspired her to found IAm Karen Small, a sanctuary where she works intimately with clients. Her mission is to guide individuals in rediscovering their essence and living life in full expression.

Outside of her professional pursuits, Karen finds solace in nature, often embarking on adventures with her loved ones. Driven by a passion for uncovering life's hidden symmetries, she continues to explore the world with curiosity and wonder.

Find her online at iamkarensmall.com.

Author Photo © Ashley Drody

ABOUT THE AUTHORS

Former corporate executive–turned–intuitive mentor **JESSICA CERATO** has been immersed in numbers for decades. As a professional numerologist and energy strategist, she translates the energy of dates, numbers, and patterns into everyday language to help you feel more confidence and joy. She lives with her family in North Vancouver, British Columbia, Canada.

With a keen mind for patterns and cycles, Jessica has cultivated a powerful intellect, initially channeling it into the world of finance. However, after spending over two decades in the corporate realm, her journey took an unexpected turn. Sensing a misalignment with her purpose, she realized that the corporate world wasn't her true path and committed to finding what was.

As the Six of Diamonds, Jessica has now fully embraced her intuition as she passionately encourages others to recognize the repeating patterns in their lives and decipher the messages encoded in numbers.

Find her online at jessicacerato.com.

Author Photo © Erica Miller

ABOUT THE AUTHORS

BETH TURNER is a mom, intuitive numerologist, psychic medium, and Reiki master who finds joy in creative self-expression. She loves all things vintage, living near the ocean, and everything we can't explain in our Universe! Her curiosity has only grown with age. She lives on Canada's West Coast.

As an Ace of Spades, it wasn't until she started looking inward and analyzing her numbers that she finally gave herself compassion and discovered her previous work experiences all had a familiar pattern: *human connection*. She realized she was most satisfied when she helped people become more joyful or empowered emotionally.

She inspires people to *human better* through mindfulness, looking inward, and courageously learning out loud. The better you become, the better everyone around you becomes.

Find her online at kelpandclover.com.

Author Photo © Nick Turner

www.ingramcontent.com/pod-product-compliance
Lightning Source LLC
Chambersburg PA
CBHW030436010526
44118CB00011B/667